Conquest vs. Survival

The Quest for Racism's Cause

by

Boyd Stockdale

Conquest vs. Survival
The Quest for Racism's Cause

FIRST EDITION
FIRST PRINTING

Printed in the United States of America
Cielo Press, Mercer Island, Washington

ISBN: 978-0-9644164-3-7 0-9644164-3-3

For additional copies or reprint permission,
contact: slsmv@comcast.net

Cover art: William Mack of AMM Creative Media

TABLE OF CONTENTS

PREFACE

Racism thrives in the United States. After decades of work societal rules have changed yet racism thrives. The societal change is a veneer that covers and hides the source of racism. Our denial of racism empowers racism. Racism will continue to damage and destroy lives as well as erode the core of who we are.

We must look to the source of racism; confront it in ourselves and in our lives. That source is our culture which arose in the sixth century, A.D. and is embodied in the King Arthur myth. We learned this culture as children from our parents and social settings. We learned the right, best and correct way to be. Most cultures are exclusive and assert that those who are different are inferior or at least misguided. Racism is embedded in us and our failure to see it, name it and confront it, nurtures it.

When we can confront racism in ourselves and our culture we can begin to understand the cultural war between a conquest culture (the dominant culture of the United States) and African American culture (a survival culture). This provides the platform for conversation, dialogue and change. From this platform we will begin to end racism. When we can confront racism in ourselves and our culture, those of us who live in privilege will recognize our privilege and the denial of privilege to the African Americans.

This is a conversation that must begin with those of us who have white privilege. There is no validity for us to suggest that African Americans should do anything. It is about our culture and our confrontation with it and ourselves. Our culture loves quests that expand our importance and pride. This particular quest is improbable. This quest will require that we give up our dominance to provide the space to be healed and reconciled. The prize of this quest is far more valuable than any we achieved in the past. Will we have the courage and integrity to engage in this improbable quest? It is from the myth of King Arthur that our culture springs and from the stories that begin and end at the round table come our values.

The Round Table

"The Round Table had been made by the famous enchanter Merlin, and on it he had exerted all his skill and craft. Of the seats which surrounded it he had constructed thirteen, in memory of the thirteen Apostles. Twelve of these seats only could be occupied, and they only by knights of the highest fame; the thirteenth represented the seat of the traitor Judas. It remained always empty. It was called the perilous seat ever since a rash and haughty Saracen knight had dared to place himself in it, when the earth opened and swallowed him up.

A magic power wrote upon each seat the name of the knight who was entitled to sit in it. No one could succeed to a vacant seat unless he surpassed in valor and glorious deeds the knight who had occupied it before him; without this qualification he would be violently repelled by a hidden force. Thus proof was made of all those who presented themselves to replace any companions of the order who had fallen.

One of the principal seats, that of Moraunt of Ireland, had been vacant ten years, and his name still remained over it ever since the time when that distinguished champion fell beneath the sword of Sir Tristram. Arthur now took Tristram by the hand and led him to that seat. Immediately the most melodious sounds were heard, and exquisite perfumes filled the place; the name of Moraunt disappeared, and that of Tristram blazed forth in light. The rare modesty of Tristram had now to be subjected to a severe task; for the clerks charged with the duty of preserving the annals of the Round Table attended, and he was required by the law of his order to declare what feats of arms he had accomplished to entitle him to take that seat. This ceremony being ended, Tristram received the congratulations of all his companions. Sir Launcelot and Guenever took occasion to speak to him of the fair Isoude, and to express their wish that some happy chance might bring her to the kingdom of Loegria." (From Bulfinch's Mythology)

And so it was, that each Knight, left that table on a quest to set things right, defeat the tyrants and all evil forces, to establish justice. And it was to that table they returned to tell the tales of their quests and to celebrate. Sir Galahad would one day take the seat perilous, and from that seat would go on the greatest quest of all, the Quest for the Holy Grail."

INTRODUCTION

American Racism 101

Why consider the issue of racism again? We have legislated it out of existence. We have open housing laws, civil rights and antidiscrimination policies. Segregation is over and schools are multiethnic and multicultural. Yet, the question is before us on a daily basis. Youth gang violence, racism charges against schools, angry voices protesting the acts of police and disquieting statistics pound us day after day.

Parade Magazine in its April 18, 2004 issue blazes the question on its cover, "Fifty years ago in Brown vs. Board of Education, the Supreme Court outlawed school segregation. Shall We Overcome?" In the article itself a startling statement is made for those who believe racism has ended. "Overcoming the damage of 200 years of racism may prove to be the most difficult of American journeys."

The Seattle Post Intelligencer carried an editorial by Bob Herbert on April 27, 2004 the title of which was "Main goal of Brown V. Board has been thwarted by regressers." He quotes Ted Shaw, who was at that time soon to become the head of the National Association for the Advancement of Colored People (NAACP) Legal Defense and Educational Fund: "We honor Brown more in principle than in practice.

We live in an era now where school desegregation is all but done. We're regressing. And no one seems to care."

Progress toward racial healing and reconciliation seems more distant than it did 20 years ago. We seem to have run out of energy, or ideas, or concern, or something, but progress seems to have halted. We live in segregated communities and schools. We are separated socially, politically and economically. What is the difference between a school in a White affluent suburb and a school in an inner city ghetto? I think we know. What happened? Why are we stuck?

Our cultural intuitive response is that African Americans need to solve their problems and get on with it. The problem is them; not us. When they learn to achieve as we achieved then the problem will be over. Our intuitive response is that we need do nothing because we cannot do it for them. It is true we can't do it for them. At the same time they cannot become us. One of the assumptions of apartheid in South Africa was that South African Blacks needed to be trained and civilized to become like White people. We know how that went and how that ended.

As White Americans we must first recognize that racism is our problem. It is not about them, nor do we have control over their lives. Our part of the solution is confronting our own racism and changing it. On the one hand, this may be something we do for them, but far more importantly, we do it for ourselves. We are prisoners of racism and we must be liberated from it. Racism destroys us. The result of such liberation will open space and opportunity for the victims of racism to find liberation as well. The starting point for us is the confrontation with our own personal racism that will end the denial.

In 1997, we traveled to South Africa. In Durbin we stayed in a bed and breakfast owned by Adrie and Eryl Brill. Their perspective as Afrikaners was revealed in the stories they told.

One evening Eryl told us about the night of the election that no doubt would result in a victory for Nelson Mandela. "As we watched the returns on the television I cradled a gun in my lap. We were convinced that the Black South Africans would riot and kill all of us. We waited. When the election of Nelson Mandela was announced, we turned off the lights and prepared ourselves for what we thought was inevitable. We knew the horrors of apartheid and knew revenge would be taken. We waited for the sound of the riot; there was only silence. We waited until dawn. We fearfully opened the curtains wondering if Black South Africans would be staring back at us. No one was there." Eryl decided to go the gate at the driveway to see what was going on. A seven foot high concrete wall surrounded their home and property, a typical amenity of houses owned by White South Africans. "Still there was no sound of a riot. As I approached the gate it occurred to me that they could be standing tight against the wall and would jump out in front of the gate when they heard me coming. The street was quiet and normal. There was no mob. It was like any other morning. We opened the gate and walked downtown. There was nothing different than any other morning. Then we heard a remarkable statement. There were no riots anywhere in South Africa; the Blacks were committed to reconciliation. I cannot tell you how humbling and powerful that was."

The fear and terror for this Afrikaner family was real, but the nonviolence of the Black South Africans forced a more powerful and important confrontation. It forced the Brilles to confront racism in themselves. In another conversation Eryl told me, "we must learn to recognize racism in ourselves, name it when we see it and refuse to let it influence our actions and decisions." It struck me that the difference between the United States and South Africa was framed by this statement. In the United States we hide it and deny it. We have placed a legal veneer over it. We don't want to talk about it nor do we want to recognize it. We want to avoid it.

Our host in Durbin was Rev. James Elias, a Presbyterian Pastor. James is English in his background. The church had resisted and fought apartheid. He told many stories of that struggle and the ways the apartheid government tried to infiltrate church meetings. James always reminded me of the complexity of South Africa and cautioned against simple answers. When I told him what I thought was the difference between the U.S. and South Africa he agreed. As he often did, he added an important insight: "We must learn to laugh at racism, while its consequences are awful, it is ludicrous and humorous." This puzzled me and James recognized my puzzlement. So he continued, "Do you understand why apartheid bankrupted the financial resources of South Africa? Think about it. Every rail depot and every airport had to have four baggage delivery systems, one for White baggage, one for Coloured baggage, one for Black baggage and one for White baggage handled by Black baggage handlers. Four baggage systems are very expensive. How could I as a White South African have ever detected that my baggage was touched by a Black South African baggage handler? Why would I care?" As he laughed I began to understand.

The same perspective was offered by a Black South African tour guide on Robbin Island. This was where Nelson Mandela had been imprisoned. All of the tour guides had been inmates in that brutal prison. As he welcomed us on the bus and introduced himself our guide said, "Black South Africans are determined to end the cycle of hatred and violence, and while we carry the scars, we will not ever seek vengeance. We know that will only create a future when someday White people will take revenge on us. It must stop here. We developed racist attitudes during apartheid; we must recognize those attitudes and name them in ourselves."

As we approached the prison he told us what it meant to be an inmate. His humor emerged immediately. "Everything was divided by color. So, White inmates got White sugar while Black and Coloured inmates got brown sugar. Maybe the White sugar would turn Blacks and Coloureds White." The absurdity of racism was once again named. The punch line of his story was, "now that we know refined sugar is worse for our health than unrefined sugar, the Blacks and Coloureds were being better cared for." His laughter was infectious.

Again and again, almost as a mantra, most everyone we met would say we must learn to name racism every time we see it in ourselves and in others, so we are able to refuse to make decisions based on it. Many of them hoped that if they named and confronted racism, someday our grandchildren may no longer live in a racist society. They are imagining that new world and it seems far less distant to them than it does to us.

Ironically, we have acknowledged racism, we have studied it and we have resolved to end it. We have failed in all of this to identify the roots of racism and consequently have failed to understand how racism works and thrives in the United States. We have been treating symptoms not the disease. We have been addressing the outward behaviors while covering the power that drives those behaviors. With that recognition our quest begins.

Martin Luther King, Jr. and school desegregation were the focus of many discussions in my high school years in Colorado. Various images are engraved in my memory.

13

Children, not much younger than I, being escorted into school by armed guards, cops in dark reflective sun glasses beating women and children, a governor standing in front of a school with a baseball bat threatening children and Martin Luther King's, "I have a Dream" speech are among them. The tranquility of the 1950's was shattered by angry voices, mass demonstrations, violent and brutal retaliation. There is nothing we resent more than change that disrupts our tranquility.

In far away Colorado, there were many voices raised against these disruptive and disturbing people and events. Some actually believed that separate but equal made sense. The fact that equal was never equal seemed appropriate to them as well. Other voices, even stronger voices supported desegregation in the South. Among these were my parents, at least in my presence. They had seen and experienced segregation at an earlier time in their lives and judged it to be unfair and unjust. At least that was my impression. As an adolescent it was difficult to separate the voices and understand the anger that was so often present in the discussion. People I had been taught to respect and admire were on both sides. My confusion about all of this arose in part as it was a rather academic and intellectual discussion. I had never met nor had a conversation with a Black person.

Adolescents often appeal to the fairness of rules. Justice, fairness and rule enforcement become very important as games are played and tests are administered. In my adolescent mind segregation seemed generically unfair and therefore ought to end. There was little other basis from which to work. I had no experience or even a clear sense of Jim Crow segregation laws.

All of this was made more difficult when for the first time I met and conversed with several African American adolescents. As the President of the Westminster Youth

14

Fellowship in the Arvada Presbyterian Church, I met the President of the WYF of the People's Presbyterian Church in Five Points as African American neighborhood in Denver. I am unable to remember her name after all these years, so I will call her Ruth. She was energetic, enthusiastic and attractive. She had a great sense of humor and the meeting we were both attending was great fun largely because of her. We decided to have a combined meeting of our two youth groups. This meant that we needed to meet together and plan the arrangements and program. Being young, neither of us seemed to understand the length of time such a process might take, nor the hurdles we might encounter. Perhaps Ruth did but I certainly didn't.

When I told my parents of these plans they seemed supportive of the idea and suggested that we host them in Arvada. I had been invited to People's Presbyterian Church and Arvada had never been proposed. So, I was noncommittal. The real concern began when I told them I needed to drive to Five Points that very night to meet with Ruth and others at her church. The response was quick and final. I could not do this. But, I said, she has many ideas and lots of energy, we could do some really fun things together. My father commented that he knew her dad and thought the world of him as well. That settled it in my mind; dad had just endorsed the idea that Ruth and I should meet together. No, he said, it was too dangerous for me to go there anytime, but especially at night. Perhaps, he suggested, she and some of them could come to Arvada. But when I called her and made this suggestion her response was the same. No, her dad would not allow this, driving to Arvada at night was too dangerous. I remember feeling very awkward about all of this, and thought she did as well. There seemed no way for us to solve the dilemma. Thinking back on it, I wonder what would have happened if we found a halfway point where we could meet that was not in Five Points, nor

Arvada. We never did meet and the combined meeting never happened. My first conscious encounter with racism was a mystery. I simply did not understand the problem.

What was the danger? I had driven all over Denver, certainly an easier task then than it now is. I had never been told to avoid areas because they were dangerous. Chances were I had already driven through Five Points. This seemed more odd to me a few weeks later when I insisted that I drive to the football game in Littleton. Littleton was across Denver about 25 miles away all on surface streets and it was snowing. My driving experience did include snow, but was rather limited. Dad told me that I should not drive because of the snow, "By the end of the game the streets will be covered with ice." When I persisted he relented and told me that I would probably have an accident, which I did. I smashed in the right front fender.

Danger seemed not to be the issue. If I could not drive to Five Points because it was dangerous, then what was I doing as an inexperienced driver driving a car much further in snowstorm? How could it be that the danger of snow and ice was less than the danger of going to Five Points? The danger had to do with who was in Five Points, not the drive to get there. Would I be attacked, beat up, robbed, or what? The answer my father offered went something like this: "Well, you know things are a bit stirred up right now. They might resent a White kid in their neighborhood." Things seemed stirred in the South but that was a long way away. Denver didn't seem stirred up. The meeting certainly wouldn't be dangerous, perhaps controversial, but the idea already was supported especially if it happened in Arvada. Was Ruth the danger? I certainly would have described her in terms that made sense to an adolescent male and might have been very alarming to his parents. Were they concerned that I might want to date her? Was she dangerous as a Black girl/woman? It was never said, and the conversation ended with, "You will not drive to Five Points, period." I had learned when the no appeal point was reached and we had reached it.

What did I learn and what was being taught? First, African Americans are dangerous people. They are unpredictable and cannot be trusted. Some may be okay, but it is not possible to reliably identify them. African American girls are not safe for White boys. Somehow innocent White boys will be tricked or deceived into a relationship that can never work or be allowed. White boys are easily seduced by Black girls and any notion of a relationship is asking for trouble. I probably had not allayed those fears in my description of Ruth.

I learned that the issues of civil rights and school desegregation were important in another part of the world but in my world it was different. The reasons for the difference would not be or could not be articulated. I was to accept this as fact because that was the way it was.

I could not have known that I was being taught from the long practiced racism manual of my culture.

"A nation is a choice. It chooses itself at fateful forks in the road by turning left or right, by giving up something or taking something –and in the giving up and the taking, in the deciding and not deciding, the nation *becomes*. And ever afterwards, the nation and the people who make up the nation are defined by the fork and by the decision that was made there, as well as by the decision that was not made there."[1]

I did not know about a fork in the road, nor did I understand it. It just was.

The mystery became deeper when I began to hear people, including my parents, say that Martin Luther King, Jr. was right. The way the Negroes (their name of that period) were treated in the South was wrong and needed to be corrected. This was often followed by a comment that deepened the mystery of it all. His work in the South was appropriate, but it would be wrong for him to come to Colorado. What was right to do in the South did not apply to Mexicans and Native Americans in Colorado. Neither had I ever met any Mexicans or Native Americans. There was a connection between my father's response to my request to drive to Five Points and concern that Dr/ King might come to Colorado. What would have been the response had Ruth been Mexican or Native American? I suspect I would have been told that I could not go, but the reasons would have been more blatantly and openly racist. The mystery of it all deepened. My adolescent "what if-ing" poked at the mystery. What if Dr. King came to Five Points? Could I go there to see and hear him? Would his presence make it less dangerous? What was the danger? What if someone like Martin Luther King came and rallied Mexicans and Native Americans? I am sure there were close family friends who feared exactly that moment and were ready to respond with violence. It was never discussed.

The darkness of the mystery only deepened as it became clearer. I was learning the "what," while the "why" remained a mystery. I realized White people do not freely associate with people of different races because those races are not to be trusted. They all represent a threat to the values of White America and it is up to White America to protect those values. I remained unclear about why this sense of threat was so persistent. At least in Colorado, White people were the majority. White people were business owners and political leaders. How had I triggered a cultural alarm by suggesting a trip to Five Points? "While the colonial slave codes seem at first sight to have been intended to discipline Negroes, to deny the freedom available to other Americans, a very slight shift in perspective shows the codes in a different light. They aimed, paradoxically, at disciplining White men. Principally, the law told the White man, not the Negro what he must do, the codes were for the eyes and ears of slave owners."[2] I was standing in a very dangerous place. I was in danger of challenging the rules of my culture and weakening that culture in the face of threat. The mandate was being declared. Keeping those undesirable people out depended upon White people maintaining the rules. I was nearing adulthood, and the time had come for me to learn.

Rock and roll was new in those days; my parents preferred Pat Boone to Elvis Presley. They failed to realize we did not see popular singers; we heard them on the radio in our cars. Television was in its infancy. We liked songs for their sound and sometimes the words. The words of some songs did tell a story and, if it connected to us that song became very popular. If the song was nonsensical and we liked the sound, we would learn the nonsensical words. We rarely had any clear sense of the appearance of the singers unless we bought the record and their picture was on the cover. One of my favorite songs on the radio was Blueberry Hill by Fats Domino. When I bought the record I realized for the first time that he was Black. This was surprising to me and I wondered what would happen when I brought it home. Mom was disturbed. She got that familiar harrumph look and said nothing. The message was clear she strongly preferred Pat Boone. Another "what-if" popped into my head. "What if" I put Blueberry Hill in a Pat Boone cover, would her response be different? I knew the answer.

The precipice that I was standing near did involve African Americans. I now know how easily an opportunity was missed. A relationship which would have introduced me to African Americans and their culture, informed me, and provided a friendship, was lost. The opportunity to form a relationship that would bring change was missed. We have missed that opportunity for 50 years, and without relationship, racial healing cannot ever take place.

The precipice, however, far more pointedly involved Mexican Americans. The stereotyping was planted firmly within me. "They are lazy, no good and dangerous people. They are an imminent threat to our way of life. We must stand solidly against them for their numbers are significant and growing." In Colorado they were the real threat, the real problem. This was the embedding of racism in my life and experience that transferred to African Americans but never as deeply or profoundly. My education and personal quest had begun although I did not realize it or even make a commitment to it. The year was 1957.

Almost fifty years later, we have had school integration, affirmative action, civil rights legislation and endless studies and forums about racism. We have had White flight, gentrification of Black neighborhoods and increasing imprisonment of Black males. We remain largely segregated socially, politically and economically. African Americans still feel fear and anger. White people are still afraid to go to Black neighborhoods at night, and Blacks are stopped by police if they enter a White suburban neighborhood at night. Many immigrants have entered the United States and succeeded while African Americans continue to struggle to achieve. After all this time, what has really changed? In the fifties and sixties there was caution that this civil rights thing would take time. Time, and more time has passed, and racism thrives. In the seventies the riots in major cities announced the end of patience, yet little changed. In the eighties the first attacks on affirmative action were launched in the courts and in the nineties affirmative action was effectively brought to an end. Lots of time has passed, but little has changed. Why is this so difficult to change? Many have worked hard and stood clearly against racism and yet it thrives. We made racism illegal, yet it thrives. We declared the issue solved and ended affirmative action, and yet it thrives. Libraries are filled with books and studies that describe the evil of racism and yet it thrives. We have film libraries filled with movies like *To Kill a Mockingbird* and still it thrives. We have experienced the Watts riots, the Black Panthers, Malcolm X and many others, and still it thrives.

Every so often a celebrity makes a racist statement. A flurry of news reports appear in newspapers and television in which the celebrity is held up for ridicule. The celebrity is chastised and often fired. Jimmy the Greek, Rush Limbaugh and Paul Hornung are a few recent examples. The celebrity usually apologizes, indicates the statement was misunderstood and life goes on. We can relax again, assured that racism has been defeated. The public execution has taken place.

We may be puzzled at such public gaffes but we are mystified by the divergent views of the O. J. Simpson trial. African Americans often believe he was set up and was innocent while White people assume he was guilty and got off because of his wealth. White people see his fame as his ticket to freedom, and Black people see it as the cause of his persecution. Black students reporting incidents of physical abuse by school officials brings a strong protest by African Americans while White Americans defend the schools and speak of discipline and responsibility.

After all these years, the chasm has only widened. It would seem that all of those efforts had minimal impact. What do we do to change it? What do we do to end racism? There is a disturbing question that lurks in the background of this society: *Is it possible to change it or end it?*

We must pay attention to how we learned racism. I learned it by another name, loyalty to my culture and way of life. I learned fear. I was denied the opportunity to confront the fear and to learn that it was false fear. I learned that it affirmed me and my opportunity to do what I wanted. I learned it because there were few if any voices naming it for what it was. I learned it because my culture had built into me the infrastructure to accept and act on the notion that White people are in fact superior to everyone who is not White. Perhaps, it was unintentional, but I had been carefully prepared and carefully taught and it worked.

This we must understand about ourselves. If we do not, changing it and ending it will be impossible. Our denial of racism and our avoidance of relationships feed and nurture it. We do not have a choice any longer. The fork in the road is before us again. The opportunity to change is before us. We must end racism. That lurking question cannot be allowed to go unanswered. Failure to end racism simply dooms all of us to loss, imprisonment and destruction. That must never be seen as an option. The failure to end racism is too costly. We must be confronted or confront ourselves if we are to ever recognize the racism that is embedded in us.

It was this that Rudy Cuellar first did for me. He was the most irritating, frustrating and threatening person I had ever met, and he was the most valued and one of the most important people in my life. As the associate pastor at First Presbyterian Church in Roseville, California, I was told that I would be responsible for organizing a Mexican American Concilio (council) in that community. There were eight Mexican American groups in town. It had been decided that the church would pay the rent on a building chosen by these Mexican American groups. This would be a place in which they could meet, organize a concilio and unite in common cause and education.

My upbringing in Colorado appeared to have some ambivalence regarding African Americans but regarding Mexican people it had been crystal clear. My reaction to this job assignment was immediate and clear. I did not want anything to do with this project. Soon the need for employment overcame my initial response.

The first meeting in this process was with Rudy Cuellar, local president of the Mexican American Political Action Committee. I am sure he knew the first time we met what he was up against. He took on the challenge and did so with amazing grace. When I did things every so often that would make him furious, he could yell at me only in Spanish. After a few minutes he would calm himself and yell at me in English. He taught me, he cajoled me, he confronted me, he irritated me and he changed me. His work took a year, but finally I began to get it. On one occasion I did something that made him so angry he set up a picket line around the church on Sunday morning. When we met before worship, the head of staff asked me how the concilio project was going. "Not so well" was my only response.

We did find a suitable building, it was renovated to meet the needs of this new concilio and it was opened. The opening night was marked by a candlelight parade through town. At the front of the parade Rudy Cuellar and I held the La Raza banner. This began my personal commitment to the quest from which I had been diverted ten years earlier. In that moment I realized racism was flourishing around me, and I had been a part of its nurture. As we paraded through town that night, I wondered what would be the response from my father. When I told him about it later, I was amazed at his openness and affirmation. It really was unintentional training I had received. The mystery of my adolescence began to come clear. Little did I know how difficult and long this quest would be.

Here we are 35 years later. We have identified systemic racism, but we have not identified its roots. We have focused on moral choice, justice, fairness, and equality. We have railed against our institutions that perpetuate the very racism we want to end. Mass demonstrations, Dr. King Birthdays, Black History Months, forums and public meetings have not moved or changed systemic racism. We have succeeded only to the degree that racism is no longer as blatant as it once was. It is more subtle now, hidden and glossed over. However, racism has changed little; its effects are still devastating. Any progress we have made ironically makes it easier for us to deny its existence.

In the 1980's and 90's a new wave of immigrants entered the United States. They came from many places representing cultures dramatically different from that of the United States. There was often resentment and racism toward them. Most of them brought a strong cultural identity and value system. Most of them brought stories and myths with them but could only share as English was learned. As I worked with these groups I realized they had something I didn't: an understanding of their culture and its cultural myth story. All that I knew of my "culture" was that I was Northern Irish. I knew that because mother told me "we wear orange not green on St. Patrick's Day." That explanation never seemed to work at school on St. Patrick's Day.

Americans seem to lack a sense of cultural identity. In fact, when asked, most reply that they don't have a culture, "I am American" is their typical response. I tried for some time to identify the cultural myth story of the United States and could not. This led me to an inquiry that convinced me that we must move this discussion to another place. The root and energy source of racism is our culture. Racism arises from our culture and is embedded in us all. We cannot be human without a culture. Racism will thrive until we identify its roots and stop responding to the energy source that feeds that racism. We must learn our own culture and our own identity. Once we have confronted racism in ourselves, then we must take the second step. The quest will become yet more uncomfortable. We must learn our culture and recognize the racism that it teaches and practices. This step will offend many of the assumptions of a culture that thrives on quests.

CHAPTER ONE

Why A Quest?

Quest is a strong and ever- present theme in Northern European Culture. The quest informs our history and most of our values. This is an invitation to enter a quest, but one that is counter intuitive to our culture. This is not a quest to conquer, or to gain power and wealth. This is a quest to understand broken relationships and why they are so difficult to repair. This is a quest to give up power and position in favor of justice and fulfillment. This is a quest to find the truth within us and to confront the evil within ourselves.

This quest sounds strange to our cultural ears. The quest is usually a way to gain power, find wealth and explore new opportunities. This invitation is to explore new opportunities that require counter intuitive initiatives. It is a quest in which we will give up some things we have valued, clutched tightly in our fists and protected at great cost.

This quest requires profound preparation. We must first understand our past and the culture that has defined that past and continues to define our present. Our past has resulted in alienation and deep hurt that continues to deepen. We are only peripherally aware of that hurt and alienation. We receive notice of it with surprise and denial. We fail to understand that our surprise and denial deepens the hurt and alienation.

When and if we understand our past, our culture and the difficulty that faces us currently, we can begin our quest. This quest will lead us into painful conversations and deep personal reflection. Our first impulse will be to abort the quest. Who wants to enter painful situations? Pleasure is far preferable to pain. Our culture thrives on pleasure and self gratification. In this quest the old platitude, "no pain, no gain" clearly applies. The gain will certainly be worth the pain. If we will enter this quest we can in time find a new world in which we learn from each other, share strength with each other and give each other fullness of life. Imagine if you can a world in which alienation no longer eats at the core of our lives, our dreams, and our abilities. Imagine a society fulfilling all of its potential and fulfilling the lives of all its citizens. Such a world is so far from us it seems almost silly.

In our culture this is a very improbable quest. Its improbability is likely the reason that the relationship between European Americans and African Americans is frozen in place. While we want this to change, and hope that it might change, it never does. We are still a segregated society socially, politically and economically. Anger and resentment boil barely beneath our surface politeness. We are so frightened of its truth that we deny its very existence. We attempt to assure ourselves we have legalized it out of existence. We want to believe that the end of legal segregation brought an end to racism. We want to believe the problem persists only in the minds of whining false victims. It is difficult for us to see that segregation and racism has changed, not gone away. Blatant images of racism and segregation in the 1950's have now become hidden and stealthy.

We are all stuck in the trap of racism, Whites and Blacks. We are so stuck that even our good intentions become part of the problem. The chasm deepens between us. Frustration on the part of those who experience racist behavior grows. What can they say when the response to them is, "I had nothing to do with slavery; you need to get over it; quit whining and achieve." This quest is one of high adventure. Can we get across that chasm? Can we build something new in the chasm that begins to fill the void? This is a quest of healing, not conquest, and may be the greatest frontier ever explored by our culture. It is a quest that will change our culture and replace an old vision with a new one.

So, people of the round table, I invite you on a quest; perhaps it is actually the quest of the Holy Grail.

CHAPTER TWO

Hypothesis

The root of racism is embedded in culture. Racism is the logical extension of learning to do things the right way, and then meeting people who do those same things differently. The obvious conclusion is that others are wrong, weird, stupid, uncivilized, etc. The result is culture clash and conflict. History is filled with the stories and events of this ethnocentricity.

My early childhood was spent in a rural area outside of Denver. I attended a two room school. Grades 1-4 were in one room and 5-8 in another. It was a wonderful childhood. I could roam around ten acres and ride a bicycle on dirt roads in any direction for as long as I wished. I could not get far enough away from home that people did not know me.

One day I was riding my bike and came to a small apple orchard. It was a hot day and an apple was very appealing. There was no fence as fences were rare in those days. The trees were easy to climb and I picked two very nice apples and sat under a tree and ate one. After a few minutes I got back on my bike and rode home. I kept one for later. When I got home, mother asked me where I got the apple and when I told her, she became rather upset. These were not my apples. Had I asked permission to take them or had I stolen them? While I was sure permission would have been granted had I asked, I had not asked. That left me with a difficult alternative. Clearly, the second option applied and no excuses could mitigate the fact I had stolen them. This was a bit of a shock to me. It didn't seem to me I had stolen anything. I just picked two apples that the owner would have happily given me. This defense was not effective. Why couldn't I pick apples that would be freely given to me? Her response was," Stockdale's don't steal." I was to return to the scene of the crime and apologize and return the apple. The apple was actually beginning to look a bit battered at this point and I doubted the owner would be much interested. However, I got back on my bike to return the apple. I knew mom would be calling the people who owned the apple trees informing them of what I had done. They would be reporting in to her later, so simply throwing the apple away along the road was not an option. I presented the apple to the owner, who acted delighted to see it, but I could tell how he really felt. He told me to just ask next time and I could have all the apples I wanted, which I already knew, but learned it didn't count until one asks each time.

Several weeks later I was riding in the same area. Two classmates were in that same orchard picking apples. I stopped and told them they should not be stealing apples. They laughed and asked me to share an apple with them. That was not an option. Repeat offenders were dealt with rather harshly in the Stockdale household. I wondered what would happen to my two friends. Later they told me that nothing happened and, in fact, they had brought some apples home to their mothers.

I remember thinking about this incident. They were wrong, but somehow for them stealing was permitted. There was this sense that Stockdales were better than that and I was glad. It struck me as weird that for them it was different. Apparently what constituted theft was not universally agreed upon. Nothing more ever was said about this incident either at home or with my two friends. This was one of many experiences learning that Stockdales were different from other people, and we did it the correct, right way. My classmates were both White and lived as I did. We continued to play together and the whole incident faded into the blur of childhood games and adventures. What if, however, those taking the apples had been strangers and had been of another race? The subtle planting of the idea that they were not good or were thieves would be implanted ready for any reinforcement that might happen. In Colorado had they been Latino, I would have certainly heard reference to Latinos being thieves and I would have had first- hand evidence of the truth of that statement. The imbedding of racism takes place in exactly this way.

Common dictionary definitions of culture usually point at common values, customs and practices which are taught to each succeeding generation. Culture is often portrayed as the music, dance, food and costumes of a people. It is also seen as the art of a people and we display it in museums. While all of these things are elements of culture, they are all results of cultural beliefs, practices and assumptions.

Culture is much more than that. The Willowbrook Report suggests the following definition:

Culture is an integrated system of beliefs (about God or reality or ultimate meaning), of values (about what is true, good, beautiful and normative), of customs (how to behave, relate to others, talk, pray, dress, work, play, trade, farm, eat) and of institutions which express these beliefs, values and customs (government, law courts, temples or churches, family schools, hospitals, factories, shops, unions, clubs, etc.) which finds a society together and gives it a sense of identity, dignity, security and continuity.

Culture organizes and makes sense of the steady stream of data and experience that floods our senses all of the time. Culture makes sense out of constantly random and disparate pieces of information and experiences that we receive. If our culture cannot provide meaning to that information then that information is either ignored or seen as abnormal or inconsequential.

In my view, there are five functions of culture that set reality into place and define our relationship to that reality. Those five functions provide the context in which we live our lives and make sense of the world around us.

The Lens

We look at our world and our experiences through the lens of our culture. We see, hear, process and understand as our culture provides the lens that organizes scattered experiences and realities to make order and sense of them. Our experience and setting have much to do with development of the lens.

For Northern European cultures, White symbolizes life, light and hope. The Puritans arrived at Plymouth Rock to build a city of light on a hill. Black is the symbol of death and grief. But this image is just reversed in Egypt. The Nile River brings silt when it floods. This silt creates the land that is productive farmland. This black soil is highly prized and the value of this land is based on the frequency of flooding; the more frequent, the more valuable. Floods increase property values. The word 'Egypt' means black dirt, and black is the color of life and hope. The white earth in Egypt is alkaline and is desert wasteland. It produces nothing. White is the symbol of mourning and death in Egypt.

The Moral Code

Our culture sets and preserves values that keep order in the community. Communities rely upon common agreement regarding rules of behavior, morals and values. Without these agreements there would be chaos. Communities provide the body of people safety and security. Without a moral code members of the community do not know who they can trust or who they can rely upon. Criminal behavior may be defined very differently from one culture to another, but each must deal with criminal behavior. Behavior that would disrupt a community in one part of the world may be of no consequence in another. Yet each will face behavior that is disruptive. Persons who behave in this way must be isolated or expelled from the community.

In some cultures adultery is a capital offense by stoning. In the United States it is often seen as an unfortunate mistake that may or may not end in divorce.

The Membership

Branding establishes who belongs to the community. Identity is drawn from being part of a specific community. Some cultures have elaborate initiation rituals to receive children into adulthood. Whether this is by elaborate ritual or simply a matter of age, the culture defines who are members of the community and provides an identity as a result. Circumcision establishes membership in the Jewish community and has done so for millenniums. In the United States entrance into the community is far more blurred for children and youth. Perhaps it is receiving a driver's license.

The Story

The culture preserves the stories, history and experiences as tradition which confirms core values. The story tells us who we are and what we have done. The story builds identity and establishes what we believe and what we do together. Etiological stories explain why things are as they are. They describe origins and meanings of origins. The core values of cultures are usually told in the stories of those cultures. It is often through story that children are introduced to the core values of a culture and why those values are so important.

It is always interesting to ask participants in a multicultural group to tell the stories they were told as children. Those stories are the easiest way to find core values of a culture. For me the story is *The Little Engine that Could.* Perseverance and hard work are core values of my culture.

The Glorification

Culture provides the codification of uniqueness and teaches us to hold our traditions with pride. The stories of heroic people and heroic times confirm why members hold it with loyalty and pride. These stories affirm the strength of each member, the sacrifices made for them and the sacrifices they will make for others.

Cultures celebrate key events that were formative and which define decision making and attitudes for decades and even centuries. World War II was just such an event for the United States. We continue to tell the stories of that war and to celebrate its events 50 years later. In Vietnam, April 27 is a day of national celebration. This is the day that the "American war of aggression ended". This event forms the identity of the nation of Vietnam and its people.

Each of these cultural functions has negative power as well as positive power. This negative side of culture is often difficult for members to see and understand.

The Lens

The lens is not interchangeable. Alternative views of reality are rejected or ignored. People from other cultures are viewed curiously at best, and as a threat at worst. Eccentric people who see reality differently are scoffed at or made fun of. If they are perceived to be harmless they are tolerated. Stories explaining how they became so odd circulate in the community. As the stories become embellished the eccentric may be seen as mysterious.

Moral Code

The moral code can be applied to the benefit of some and the loss of freedom for others. The moral code can be the basis determining who is inferior and who is superior. Native Americans saw the land as a sacred trust that no one ever could own. The White settlers took possession and built fences around the land. The rules condemned Native Americans to reservations of useless land. Native Americans were a threat, viewed as savages who could easily be manipulated.

Values in a particular historical situation are not necessarily the same in another. Gunfights on Main Street were common in the Old West. Dueling was common in the East before that. Today we have drive-by shootings them. Dueling, gun fights, and drive by-shootings are all illegal now.

The moral code continues to reflect the context in which it exists. Slavery was defined as moral until 1861 in the United States. The moral code changed, slavery was ended and the Civil War followed. The behavior toward former slaves continued to repress and subjugate. Slavery was outlawed but it took 100 years to guarantee voting rights for African Americans.

Membership

Identity can become egocentric and ethnocentric. The community is an enclave. Ethnocentricity provides the means for one culture to oppress another. Culture is isolated, either as a result of geography, exclusion by another culture, or by becoming exclusive. Ethnocentricity is a primary building block that fosters and nurtures racism. As the community grows inward, the outside threats become magnified, which results in deepening fear. As fear deepens, focus shifts to identity within the culture. The values and power of the culture become exaggerated to provide self assurance and confidence. The more the community grows inward, the greater the sense of threat from those outside. The fear within will demand uniformity and those who are different will become targets for exclusion and oppression.

Nazi Germany is an example of this pattern. And as did Nazi Germany, these inward growing communities become a threat to all those around them.

The Story

History and experiences are remembered differently as time passes The events of history that contribute to pride and loyalty become idealized, the errors and weaknesses of heroes minimized. The events of history that were painful, the failures and the defeats, get left behind or explained away. Our ability to learn from history, learn from the mistakes of the past diminishes.

Did George Washington throw a silver dollar across the Potomac? Who died in the Alamo, White men or Mexican Nationals?

The Glorification

Uniqueness becomes exclusivity: we/they. Difference is neither trusted nor respected, but is viewed as wrong and inappropriate. The willingness to inter Japanese citizens in detention camps during World War II is a good illustration. The fear of a Japanese invasion drove the United States to ignore its own Constitution.

This is the root of racism. We are right and superior to everyone. We know the best way to do everything and everyone must learn our way. If they do not they are stupid and disposable. If they learn to live as we tell them we might let them into the membership of our culture. This, however, will cost them their identity and culture. Their new identity will be their way into membership. Traces of the old identity will perpetuate their exclusion. Assimilation is the only way.

We learn all of this, our culture and language, as small children. Small children mimic sounds and learn to speak. Words begin to have meaning, verbal communication begins and the vocabulary grows. Children in English-speaking places learn that adjectives precede nouns and nouns usually precede verbs, long before they know there are such things as adjectives, nouns and verbs. They learn this by listening and through correction by parents. Children in Spanish speaking places learn that the noun precedes the adjectives and in German they learn the verb comes at the end of the sentence. They learn by listening and being corrected. Amazingly children at a young age can learn several languages this way. It is not until they begin to write the language that grammar is important for them to know.

The same is true for cultural values and traditions. Children are told to do tasks and behaviors the correct way, and will be corrected until they do. Many of the foundational tasks are completed by age 6. This is vital for the development of children and our culture provides the means to make sense of the chaos of information, experiences and events that surround them. This establishes their relationship to that reality. This primary function sets the stage for ordering human relationships, societal patterns, organizational assumptions and the role of institutions and organizations.

As children we learn these rights and wrongs in very subtle ways. When as children we were told to do something or not do something we likely asked "why?" The answer was often "because," or, "because I am your parent." It is likely our parents did not know why either; they just knew it was the correct way to behave. We learned these behaviors without explanation most of the time. Why do we shake hands? Why always with the right hand? There are cultural reasons, but it is unnecessary to know those reasons. We just know it is right. It is not necessary to know that a sword would be drawn by the right hand from the left side of the body. If a person extended an empty right hand then they could not draw their sword. Left handed people were often looked upon with disdain, and maybe this is one of the reasons. Along with the hand shake, children in this culture are told to look the other person straight in the eye. This indicates respect and truthfulness.

Many Asian cultures do not shake hands but bow in respect; and to look another person in the eye is very disrespectful. This difference of greeting was seen as strange and wrong in the United States, resulting in an early stereotype of Asian people as inscrutable, sneaky and unreliable.

It is in these very types of transactions that we identify difference as negative. It is easy for us to become suspicious and even judgmental. Biases, prejudices and stereotypes arise that explain the ways in which others are weird, stupid, greedy, or lazy; the list goes on and on. Interchanges are opportunities to confirm that those prejudices and stereotypes are correct. They become accretions like barnacles on dock pillars. In short, we racialize relationships and events, behaviors and attitudes. We conclude that it is unnecessary to ever meet or know a person of another race or culture. We already know everything we need to know about them. This is the birthplace of racism.

It is a very short step to assume that those weird and stupid people who do things so differently than we do are in fact inferior and perhaps not even human. "Almost without exception, colonizers based their enterprises on the claim that the colonized were biological and cultural inferiors."[1] Racism, slavery and even genocide all become possible. The lens through which reality is defined sets in motion the legitimization of attempted or actualized dominance of one people over another. The culture that dominates may not even be in the majority of the population. The culture that dominates controls resources, wealth and power as the claim of superiority is established. So it was in South Africa. Ten percent of the population enforced Apartheid against the remaining 90 percent.

Racializing becomes racism when the "others" do not evidence affirmation of the core values of the dominant culture. Dominance is often social and economic, which becomes political power. Core values define relationships, success and lifestyle. For example, Northern European culture values hard work, initiative and material wealth. When we view a culture that is not materialistic through our lens we respond immediately. Many who travel to poverty-stricken areas of the world are surprised and amazed that people who have nothing seem to be very happy. The surprise indicates inconsistency with our culture values. Lacking money in our culture defines happiness. It does not occur to people to ask what these poverty-stricken areas recognize as the source of happiness.

This question is a curiosity for travelers: it becomes much more urgent when people from those places immigrate to the United States. The curiosity about their happiness is now defined by their willingness to find happiness our way. If they do not immediately seek wealth producing opportunities through hard work, our culture will determine that they are lazy and have no ambition. When immigrants arrive in this country and do not speak English there is an expectation they will somehow get a job immediately, work hard and begin to succeed. They must learn English in the first couple of months or they are judged to be unwilling or incapable. This judgment comes from people in this country who have never even attempted to learn another language.

Some immigrant cultural groups are more easily accepted than others. In each case these cultures value strong business skills, have financial resources and are materialistic. These cultures achieve in schools and in the community because they work hard and are usually accommodating to our culture. People will say, "They fit in."

Some cultures are resisted and even rejected as they insist on keeping their own culture intact and strive to maintain their language in their family. They are willing to live on less income and use work time to care for family. Their achievement does not fit the standard definition of our culture. They achieve but not by material standards. Their cultural core values do not focus on accumulation. They live in tension with our culture and it shows. People will say, "They don't fit in."

Appearance is a primary value in North American culture. All cultures define beauty. North American culture defines it in very specific ways. We have constant reminders of the prototype of "the beautiful people". They are movie stars, models, athletes and very successful people. Clothing fads come and go; you are in or you are out. The beautiful people establish the fashion styles as well as lifestyles. Ironically, a bronzed look is prized which means tanning booths and various lotions are big business. It is ironic that White people want to become brown to achieve beauty when brown people are often not accepted in the society at large. Skin color with the correct body type and facial features is attractive. Pale white looks sickly, yet African Americans have tried to look whiter in order to fit in.

We want to be with attractive people and avoid being in groups that are not attractive. We want to look good and be with people that look good. We may affirm that an unattractive and poorly dressed person could be a good person, but we are unlikely to find out. We will not be drawn to searching for the good in that person, but will aggressively seek the good in an attractive person.

How did we learn this stuff? Where do these stereotypes and assumptions come from? As an adolescent boy, I knew an attractive girl when I saw one. When was the prototype installed? Today it certainly is reinforced by television and movies. In my childhood television did not exist. I did regularly go to the Saturday afternoon matinees at the movie theater where the Western Cowboy was the primary genre. Hopalong Cassidy, Red Ryder, the Lone Ranger and Tonto as well as Gene Autry were the best known to me. I did not know the meaning of "Tonto" until I learned Spanish. Did the movie makers intend to call the Native American, "Fool"? It's true they were often rescuing some fair maiden but I was not focusing on the fair maiden or at least I didn't think I was. Somewhere around age 13 or 14 that focus began, but I was already operating with the profile at that point. Gradually, Saturday movies, pictures in magazines and comments that someone was attractive or unattractive set the profile without any conscious involvement on my part.

My father was a printer who was probably a frustrated farmer. He loved owning land and raising crops. He worked hard all of his life and did whatever was required to support a family. Mom and Dad even owned a small business for a few years. He spoke often of hard work and being a good worker. His experience was that being a hard worker was the only way one could achieve. He often reminded me that nothing of value was free. All good things required hard work. As a child I had chores to do which I often neglected or tried to neglect. It was in the neglectful moments that Dad's foundational lecture was repeated. I know very well the source of the hard work prototype that has influenced my life. It is still a voice that speaks inside my head.

These prototypical values have often been the point at which people were stereotyped. Those who did not work hard would never achieve anything. They would always be lazy no-accounts and nothing would change it. In my upbringing it remains unclear whether such stereotypes were ever openly attached to any particular ethnic group as a blanket statement. It is clear, however, that the connection was made without my conscious acknowledgement because it was one of the centerpieces of my racism regarding Mexicans and Native Americans.

Culture is established in exactly this way. Definitions of truth, assumptions about correct living, values, appropriate social customs and profiles of good people and bad people are all installed in us. We are not often even aware of the installation and may never become consciously aware of them. We are simply doing what we were taught and doing it the correct, right and appropriate way.

It is this that brings the huge surprise to White people in the United States. All of that stuff that has been installed is filled with racist assumptions and beliefs. We are not even aware of it and will deny it while affirming at an intellectual level that racism is evil and must be ended. Steps we will take to end racism are in themselves racist acts. We may become paternalistic. We want African Americans to succeed. We do not want racism to persist. We will work very hard to help them. We will recognize that they are okay when they become us. There is no respect for them, their identity, culture or values. They are not adults; they are children and we just need to raise them up. How shocking it is to White people trying to be helpful to be told they are racists. Our denial and defensiveness is massive. The White people probably leave in anger believing that Blacks can't be helped as they hear a small voice suggesting inferiority. The Blacks leave once again saying, "White Folks just don't get it."

It is common for White people to assume that African Americans do not have a culture distinct from the culture of the United States. The logic goes something like this: They were forced into White culture as slaves and while slavery was a bad thing, they did learn our culture. They have lived in this culture for 300 years, have worked here, have been educated here and have participated socially here. The next observation often made reveals the racism. "Why don't they do better here? What is wrong with them?" Or, sure slavery was bad, but I didn't have anything to do with that. They just need to get over it and quit playing the victim role.

This lack of awareness begins the cycle again. The failure to recognize African American culture is born out of our own culture. Our culture is the correct one and therefore if they have one it is obviously wrong, bad, and pathological or they would have achieved by now. Achievement is what it's all about. If they have a culture and it blocks achievement, then it needs to be changed.

An early difficulty in identifying our own racism is understanding the types or categories of racism. If we understand racism as the behavior of White supremacist groups, then we are clearly anti-racist and abhor racism. Racism, however, expresses itself in a much wider range of behaviors. What are the categories of racism?

- Blatant Racism in which a person believes they and their race are by definition superior to another and have the inherent right to control them. The glorification of the culture is taken to an extreme that includes racial purity. The examples of this are the Ku Klux Klan and other White Supremacy groups.

- Intentional Racism in which a person practices racism knowingly for their own self interest and is unwilling to acknowledge the consequences of their behavior. "We must protect our neighborhood and our families. "We know that those people tend to be criminal by nature. "It's just the way it is. Racial profiling for police departments, the practice of redlining in real estate, discriminatory practices in employment, de facto segregation in schools are just a few examples.

- Uninformed Racism in which a person lives out the values of their own culture, recognizing its values and affirming them without reflecting on the consequences for persons of other cultures. They hold their cultural values with such loyalty it has never occurred to them that it might be flawed in anyway. Racism is not an issue; it is just that those people don't measure up. The racism is benign in the sense that they may wish that they could change those people and they do not express aggressive or destructive behaviors against them. Example: African Americans have the same culture as ours; they just need to get over it.

- <u>Unintended Racism</u> in which people do not recognize the racism that is imbedded in their world view or their cultural perspective and who see themselves as opposing racism. A failure to understand their own cultural sources prevents them from hearing the accusation of being racist. They intellectually have chosen not to be racist. The pain of listening to their racist behavior prevents them from being able to identify the source of their racism and an ability to overcome it in themselves. This requires a confrontation in which they will not or cannot deny their own racism. This is the most common example of racism in White Americans.

These are placed in reverse order of difficulty to address. Race supremacy is the easiest; it is the most obvious and a wide consensus has arisen since seeing the horror of the outcome. Intentional racism is a series of obvious acts that can be changed by policy and law. Uninformed racism is more difficult, for we must find ways to help people to see the flaws in that which they think is perfect. If safe settings can be found in which education can take place, this can be changed. The most difficult is the unintentional racism for the confrontation will be painful and difficult. It is however, the most hopeful for these people have already made the intellectual commitment.

Bishop Desmond Tutu's question confronts all of these types of racism. "How was it possible for normal, decent, and God-fearing people, as White South Africans considered themselves to be, to have turned a blind eye to a system which impoverished, oppressed, and violated so many of those others with whom they shared the beautiful land that was their common motherland?"[4]

If we understand how culture works, then we must understand our own culture, its source and its myth story. Failure to understand the source of our culture and its values prevents us from seeing and understanding the racism that is implanted in us. We cannot defeat racism until we learn to not act on it or make decisions based on it. First we must understand our own culture and second we must understand the racism that is imbedded in us by that culture. The conflict between two cultures, both intentional and both with strongly held value systems are in direct conflict with each other. This conflict is more than just a culture clash; this is a conflict of wills. The conflict itself reasserts and solidifies racism. This has not been addressed in practical, relational ways and it is to this that we must turn our attention. This is the third major step in our improbable quest. We must recognize the cultural conflict and confront it. It will take courage, patience and careful listening. It will be painful but it will be filled with hope.

CHAPTER THREE

The Dominant Culture of the United States

A Conquest Culture: Arthurian Cycle of Stories

The first time I wondered about the myth of my culture was in the mid 1980's. Rev. Ninh Van Nguyen introduced me to Vietnamese Culture as we drove to Fresno from Sacramento. As we talked I realized that I could not tell Ninh the cultural myth story of my culture. I thought of stories like Paul Bunyan but none of them seemed likely. These stories were all too narrow in focus to apply. I wondered if the stories of early America form that myth. What about the heroic stories like George Washington throwing a coin across the Potomac and not lying about the cherry tree? Again these seemed unlikely possibilities. The Greek and Roman myths were appealing options, but those stories seemed distant with only tangential relationships to the culture that I called my own.

I began collecting myth stories of many cultures with which I was working. All of them were cohesive and informative. Knowing those stories provided explanation for the cultural values being lived by those very people. Such a story for my culture was still allusive.

I began to wonder if I missed some obvious story in my childhood. Perhaps others could name that story. I began an exploration to find those who could tell me what I had missed. It was bewildering to ask members of my culture to name its values. Many times people responded, "We don't have a culture, we are Americans." More bewildering were the responses that listed the Bill of Rights. The most ironic response was that America is a melting pot and therefore, by implication, our culture is amorphous. My experience had been that the melting pot was indeed a myth. The melting pot was able and willing to melt Northern Europeans into one group, but refused to do so with people of color.

No wonder so many people find it difficult to relate across cultural and racial lines. To enter relationships in which people are very clear about their cultural values and identity is very threatening to those who are not clear about their own. How do we connect to another person's culture without knowing our own and without knowing to what we are connecting? Ignorance as bliss is highly overrated generally but becomes paralyzing in this case.

In 1995, my wife Sue and I went to England, she on a choir tour and me to discover the ways in which multicultural and multiethnic realities were being addressed there. Maybe the root point of my culture would have found ways to engage a variety of culture that would be instructive. I hoped that in the roots of that culture I might find the roots of my own.

Early in my conversations in England the cultural myth story became apparent. I had met with the Director for Multicultural Education in Norwich. He asserted that the culture of the United States and Great Britain were from the same myth and that the myth was retold and reaffirmed on a daily basis in both places. He was surprised that I did not realize that the myth of King Arthur and the Knights of the Round Table is the cultural myth of Northern Europeans. I was skeptical, particularly around the idea of its daily affirmation. Later I was told the same thing at York

University. I was told to buy a book of Arthur stories and, when I returned to the United States to keep track of references to King Arthur on a daily basis. I read the stories and recognized the obvious links to the culture of the United States.

The night we returned home we turned on the TV to watch the news. The first news item involved a pill that had resulted in weight loss for pigs and was now to be tested on humans. The newscaster said, "If this works it will be the Holy Grail of the diet industry." The news broke for commercials and the first commercial was for a vacuum sweeper named Excalibur. For the next week I tried to keep track of Arthur references. There were at least five to ten per day. There it was right in front of me and it had been there all along. Telling the story of King Arthur was taking place on a regular basis but I had missed it. Culture works subliminally; I knew that, now I knew how completely hidden it can be.

The cycle of stories that represent King Arthur, the Knights of the Round Table and Camelot are all part of the cultural myth that arose in Celtic Culture. This story has been told and retold and continues to live in our own time. It is instructive to realize the number of times Camelot has been done on Broadway and in film. John F. Kennedy's presidency was idealized as Camelot. Bill Clinton tried to portray that same theme. In 2004, Arthur was back as a movie and a major production by the History Channel.

The exploration of the world and the colonization of the New World were all quests for Camelot, the Holy Grail, the Fountain of Youth. The Westward movement under the mandate of manifest destiny was a movement to find gold, prosperity, and a new life. We love telling the stories of that amazing quest.

The appeal of Arthur is still with us.

- California has at various times tried to portray itself in these terms. The land of adventure, discovery and opportunity blaze through its identity.

- Cities describe themselves as Camelot as do restaurants and shopping malls.

- As the Women's Movement took root, the references to this myth became common: "Chivalry is dead. Women don't want to be saved by Knights on white horses. Men hold power by taking care of women. Women must take care of themselves."

"It is not just a romance tale. It is an epic tale that lives on in many forms. Arthur of course is a shape-shifter, passing through transformations. To diagnose the spell of his legend we must ask what is the constant, the active ingredient in all versions? I would define it as the long-lost glory or promise which is not truly lost."[5]

Remarkably it is a search for an idyllic past in the future. It is a quest to find the golden age once lost by pushing into the future, to create it again, to find the setting for it and to live it once again.

This is not just a series of stories; this is a myth that informs, empowers and fuels an entire culture. It is creative, adaptable and open-ended which allows retelling and redefining. The appeal remains even though it is unclear whether King Arthur was an historical figure. He most likely was not but was the extension of a King who defeated the Saxons.

Geoffrey Ashe in _The Discovery of King Arthur_ makes a strong case that Arthur was derived from King Riothamus who defeated the Saxons at the battle of Baden Hill and reigned from 454 AD to 470 AD. He was the Fifth Century.

To the question "was King Arthur Real?" we now have an answer. "The Arthur of Geoffrey and the romancers is a legend. But he was a real original. The British High King was in Gaul. This was the person Geoffrey and others are speaking of when they speak of Arthur."[6]

He no doubt did some outstanding things in his day as a king but certainly not all that is in the myth story. In fact the myth story grew around him and was built over time. It is likely that this story was not fully developed until the Twelfth Century, though he was King in the Fifth Century.

Even a cursory glance at the British Empire reveals the persistence and constancy of the Arthurian myth. "Here is a spellbinding, indestructible theme, national, yet transcending nationality. For better or worse it has affected the history of the country where it began. It has survived eclipses and demolitions, and Britain cannot be thought of without it."[7] This is why people in Norwich and York pointed to Arthur when I asked the question of our cultural myth. This story came to the United States on the Mayflower, took root and has become the cultural myth of the United States.

This is a powerful story because it is easily adapted to many different contexts. King Arthur and the Knights of the Round Table arose in Celtic Culture in the Fifth Century. The story has been told and retold, enhanced, amended and polished for fourteen hundred years. The retelling continues vividly in our day. In the story telling of the United States Arthurian themes constantly present themselves. Consider the American Westerns or the introduction of Superman which sounds a lot like the oath of the Round Table or the destiny themes in movies like *Sleepless in Seattle*, most of the police dramas, the Stallone movies, and on it goes. The Arthurian cycle continues even though the context in which it lives has changed. New settings are created with new costumes. The Star Wars trilogy is an amazing transformation of a Sixth Century story. Excalibur becomes a sword that is a beam of light. Arthur, Galahad, Lancelot and Guinevere are all there. The court is space, the costumes are not medieval, but it is the myth of King Arthur told again.

The dominant culture of the United States is rooted in this myth. It is the source of our culture and the values we hold. It is our culture. We must learn it and bring it from our subconscious minds. Our failure to understand the power of this myth in our lives prevents us from recognizing the very factors that inform our own racism.

Cultures enshrine stories that explain why things are the way they are. Some of these stories are etiological. The great, chosen leader must accomplish miraculous tasks like pulling the sword from the stone. No one else could complete such a feat. Other stories involve great acts on the part of common individuals. Gareth was a rag-tag boy who joined the Round Table by great acts of will and courage. Only one person could pull the sword from the stone, but many can achieve if they work hard and have courage. In all cases the Knights stand for truth, justice and courage. The stories are most easily found as children's stories, which should not surprise us.

The dominant culture of the United States has inherited and has cherished this cultural myth story from England. It is the story that we are reminded of on a daily basis. For many, it is a story they have never read and yet know of the Holy Grail, Merlin, Galahad, The Round Table, The Lady of the Lake and The Sword in the Stone. How is this possible? Those stories permeate our lives to such a degree that we may know the stories without having read them.

Yet, I have found that few African Americans know these stories or identify with them. These are not their stories nor do these stories reflect their experience or values. The notion that African Americans share our culture is discredited by this fact alone.

What are some of the primary reference points that link cultures formed by the King Arthur?

The Round Table

This was an exclusive society to which a Knight was admitted only when he had fulfilled an "adventure" or quest. The quest had resulted in saving a community from oppression or evil, overcoming the treachery of evil tricksters, or demonstrating high moral principles and unusual bravery. While the Round Table was a limited democracy, it was democracy for Knights only; others need not apply. Persons who did not fit the stereotype could not be seated as Knights. Non Celtic persons or persons of color were not seated at the Round Table. The oath taken by the Knights required that they stood for justice, fairness and good deeds. They don't claim to leap tall building and travel at the speed of bullets because neither existed in their time.

The round table, however, was less a governmental function and more a community celebration. Knights returned to the Round Table to share their stories of adventure most commonly on Shrove Tuesday. Grand celebrations took place here. Arthur was the King and he made most of the decisions. Knights responded to his call to honor and off they went on their adventures.

Most of the adventures are by individuals out to prove their honor. This is an individual exercise. The Round Table is a community gathering of individuals. It is instructive to note that families are not a major feature of this myth and, in fact, child rearing often has some rather unusual characteristics. Galahad, for example, was the son of Lancelot, which was only known by Merlin. Merlin sequestered Galahad until the moment when he would arise as the person who would seek the Holy Grail. Sending male children to be raised outside the family of origin was common.

The Round Table is about power. Power is held by a small group in comparison to the society at large. Power is tightly contained as Knights are predestined to their seats around that table. Their name is emblazoned on the seat before they arrive. There is one seat held for the purest and most noble Knight, the hero who will go on the ultimate quest for the Holy Grail. This is a table at which heroes and the superhero gather.

To gain access to the Round Table requires worthiness which is earned through competition with other Knights. No conquered people are allowed; they have been saved from some evil, but they are not admitted to the seats of power. We hear this same assertion ringing during the first Constitutional Convention of the American colonies. Only those who owned property were worthy and therefore allowed to exercise power. It was not until the Civil Rights Act in the Johnson administration that all citizens were granted the right to vote.

The myth portrays a rather naïve understanding of power. There seems to be little recognition of the corruption of power. The corruption of power did result in the death of Arthur and the demise of Camelot. This did not change the telling of the myth in idealized and even utopian portrayals. Is it possible that in every Presidential election in the United States we are still hoping Arthur will emerge as a candidate?

Values associated with the Round Table
1. Individualism
2. Fairness
3. Justice

4. Community Values, not familial values
5. Honor and respect are earned.
6. Women are weak figures who depend upon Knights to save them from evil.

Men/Women Relationships

Men and women are attracted to each other most frequently on the basis of physical appearance and little else. In fact, the superficiality of these "relationships" is striking. The Knight sees an attractive woman, decides to rescue her or marry her, and when he is successful, they ride off into the sunset. There are stories of maidens finding attractive Knights who then conspire to gain their attention. Often both seem rather narcissistic. There are some brutal stories of the treatment of women over simple misunderstandings as in the story of Geraint and Enid. There are also stories involving ugly women who will provide a test as to whether the Knight will save her as in Sir Gawaine and the Green Knight. The role of wives is betrayed in The Marriage of Arthur and Guinevere. Arthur needed to be civilized and she was perfect for the task.

Values associated with men/women relationships

1. Men are strong, silent and stoically endure.
2. Women are demur, weak and sometimes the prize of victory.
3. Relationships are superficial and often narcissistic.
4. Beautiful women and handsome Knights are the basis of romance. Romance follows attraction.
5. Women may be treated in brutal ways.
6. Adultery is a mark of impurity. The penalty is that only the purest Knight can seek the Holy Grail. Lancelot was disqualified, though he

continued to be honored and revered at the Round Table.
7. Promiscuity by single young men is expected and only slightly frowned upon.
8. Men are crude and women civilize them.

Knighthood

A person became a Knight through competition. There was no other way for this to be achieved. This competition was one-on-one, either within the community or in defeating an evil Knight in combat. The object of the competition was often to impress women, and sometimes women were held hostage and were the prize of the victor. A person may be born to a high station, but still must achieve Knighthood by this same method. Some stories tell of the well-born Knight who masquerades in lowly costume until he succeeds to the Knighthood. Other stories tell about a person born of lowly station who overcomes through great bravery and courage. Knights are greatly rewarded by wealth and this is likely to be an important motive in saving damsels in distress. Knights had to be worthy to be seated at the table. One seat remained empty waiting for a very special Knight of highest honor. The Seat Perilous was finally taken by Galahad, the only Knight pure enough to seek the Holy Grail.

Values associated with Knighthood

1. Competition determines worth and status.
2. Combat is honorable both as recreation and in conquest.
3. Right will overcome wrong. Good will prevail over evil.
4. Courage outweighs birthright, provided one is Celtic.

5. Materialism and wealth are highly prized. Those who are good will be rewarded and therefore be wealthy.
6. People are valued for what they do, not who they are.

The Role of Magic

Merlin is a Shaman, half spiritual being and half soothsayer. He sounds Christian at times and even reflects some Christian attitudes. However, these attitudes always seem somewhat artificial and are more likely to be attached to Jesus in magical connotations. The Holy Grail is one such example. The Grail must be rescued from the hands of the infidels, but one is never quite sure what will happen if it is. The stories of the Holy Grail, Excalibur and the Lady of the Lake all have a New Age religious quality. The relationship between the church and the Arthurian Court is not clear. The church is almost absent from the Arthur cycle, though the Knights are defined as Christian and often do something that seems religious. The magic of witches is much more common and much more clearly defined. It is accurate to say that the Christian presence was imposed upon the old Celtic Myth and therefore is not well integrated into the stories.

Values associated with magic/religion

1. Religion is valued but not deeply influential in life decisions.
2. Religion and magic are nearly the same.
3. There are forces that control destiny, some good and some bad, a basic dualism. Fate and the fates are in control of one's future.
4. The Grace of God is earned by good deeds and heroic action.
5. Jesus and all that he touched are magic.

The Holy Grail is imbued with the magic to heal every pain, hurt and ill. So powerful is it that a person who is not absolutely pure will be destroyed by it if they find it.

This is only a very sketchy summary of the many issues and values that are imbedded in the Arthurian cycle of stories. They are persistent in the dominant culture of the United States and represent the core values of this culture.

The Dominant Culture of the United States

When we consider the values of the Arthur myth, we can readily see the culture in which we live. It is a culture that has a history of conquest and exploration. It is a culture that has a powerful influence and yet functions undercover. Those most benefited by it are often the least aware of it.

It is a non syncretistic culture. It assumes that all cultures will be subsumed by it and absorbed into it. People are accepted when they learn to do things correctly and adopt the values of this culture. Those that resist or refuse to be absorbed are excluded. It does have some of the qualities of the Borg in the television series, Star Trek. "Resistance is useless, you will be absorbed."

The quest is a central theme. The exploration, the conquest is at the very center of these stories. How long can we resist sending people to Mars and beyond? Robots may tell us about Mars, but we will send people because only people can fulfill the quest.

We continually look for new worlds to explore. The space exploration quest is still the most ambitious, but when it receded in the news in the 80's and 90's we turned our attention to the ocean. Deep submersibles began to appear and new discoveries were made. The quest is always about finding something: streets paved with gold, the fountain of youth, the Holy Grail or land to occupy and settle. It is not surprising that quest has frequently become conquest, for when we find the treasure, we will conquer and control it. We may call it liberation, or spreading democracy, but it is what it is.

We will make all things right. We began with the Crusades and have continued to colonize, invade and control ever since. Those who need to learn our ways in order to have a good life are welcomed if they are willing to be controlled in the process. If they resist learning the right way then they are an enemy, a threat, or stupid and inferior.

So it is with immigrant groups. Those who are willing to be assimilated eventually may be allowed into the quest. Those not willing are isolated, rejected and excluded from the quest. This culture takes delight in the fact that all immigrant children will learn English and our ways through our schools. Their culture of origin becomes a footnote in their lives as they assume the values of this culture. Failure on their part to follow this pattern will impoverish them.

Historically this culture has received Northern European immigrants most easily. These groups are Caucasian and share many of the same primary values with some variations. This is illustrated by the apparent belief that a study of culture is to look at native costumes, food, music and dance. These variations are interesting or curious as long as the primary values are constant. The melting pot myth was applied easily. Dutch, German, English, Irish, Scandinavian, Italian, Polish and others gave up their national cultures and languages to become a new nation together, a new White nation.

On the other hand, it has been much more difficult for this culture to receive people of color: African, Asian, Native American and Hispanic. They look very different and do not share common values, at least not values from the same source. The melting pot never was willing to truly absorb or receive people of color with primary cultural differences. For some of these groups acceptance does start to take place in the second, third and fourth generations, as those generations adopt this culture. The fact that they still look different delays the acceptance, but in time that begins to be overcome by their work ethic and family life. Often this acceptance results from their academic and economic success. These successes are often grudgingly admired.

For other groups who do not readily adopt this culture and do not succeed academically or economically acceptance never takes place. Stereotypes develop and are embellished. Generation after generation is seen as lazy, inferior and inadequate.

Native Americans and African Americans are two particular groups never able to receive acceptance in a general or inclusive way. Both carry a similar attitude; they maintain their culture and will not assimilate. Both cultures represent active opposition to assimilation. Native Americans have held their own cultures in an increasingly complex society. This has isolated them and impoverished them. Taking advantage of the impulse to gamble may overcome the poverty, but do they lose their culture in the process? African Americans continue with a strong culture having come through slavery, segregation, Jim Crow laws, unequal education and economic deprivation. African Americans remain a primary target of stereotypes and racism. We will look at this culture in the next chapter.

How far will our culture go to coerce or dominate others? Eugenics as a movement swept through the scientific community in the first half of the Twentieth Century. Eugenics and social Darwinism were the logical outgrowths of Charles Darwin's Theory of Evolution. At least it was the logical extension in this culture. If all life evolved from lower forms to higher forms, then it must be possible to control that evolutionary process into the future. The future could be improved and the quality of life made better by removing from the future those who are defective now. In order to make that happen, procreation that extended defects would have to be stopped. The genetic background of individuals would need to be determined prior to allowing them to have children. It would provide the way for intelligence to be increased by removing people of lower intelligence from the equation. This meant sterilization on a mass scale and perhaps even banning marriages. The genetic makeup of the society would be strengthened by preventing some from procreation while intentionally bringing intelligent people together for procreation.

This idea became a movement that was supported by some very famous people. Oliver Wendall Holmes, Margaret Sanger, Winston Churchill, George Bernard Shaw, who was an eugenics extremist, Bertrand Russell, Andrew Carnegie and the Carnegie Institute, the University of California, Berkeley, New York University and many others were deeply engaged in this movement.

Eugenics began in England and spread to the United States where it received major financial and political support. Family records began to be kept and states enacted mandatory sterilizations. Mental defects were the first target of concern followed by inherited diseases, epilepsy and on and on. Anyone who was considered to be a drag on the purification of the race would need to be removed from the genetic stream. Always present in this movement was the concern for racial purity, Nordic purity to be precise. "The racial purity and supremacy doctrines embraced by America's pioneer eugenicists were not the ramblings of ignorant, unsophisticated men. They were carefully considered ideals of some of the nation's most respected and educated figures."[8]

While many groups were targeted, the one that drew special attention were African Americans. Charles Davenport, one of the early leaders of the movement, wrote to the Carnegie Institute for a grant. Drawing on his belief in raceology, Davenport offered the Carnegie trustees an example he knew would resonate: "We have in this country the grave problem of the Negro, a race whose mental development is, on the average, far below the average of the Caucasian."[9]

Racism was politely hidden under the guise of preventing disease and the consequences of birth defects. In the early 1900's, Walter Plecker was hired as county health officer in Elizabeth County, Virginia. He was simply a racist. Plecker's passion was for keeping the White race pure from any possible mixture with Black, American Indian or Asian blood. Plecker declared in a Health Bureau pamphlet, "The White race in this land, is the foundation upon which rests its civilization, and is responsible for the leading position which we occupy among the nations of the world."[10] To what did Plecker refer in this statement? What is this civilization that he defines in terms of global dominance? He asserts that this civilization occupies the "leading position" in the nations of the world and that civilization rests on the White race. Plecker may not have ever realized that this is less a discussion of a civilization than the presentation of a culture born in the Sixth Century that became Camelot.

Eugenics may seem bizarre and an archaic ancient idea, however, it did mark the first half of the Twentieth Century. The forces that nourished it are in the culture of King Arthur. Forces of exclusivity and superiority fed this movement. The goal was the creation of The Aryan Race. This movement attracted the attention of Adolf Hitler who was as well interested in a pure super Nordic race. The insanity of Adolph Hitler was born in England and nurtured to adulthood in the United States. The holocaust was born here and executed in Germany. This is a scary fact.

"Eugenics lost favor when the concentration camps were discovered and eugenics became geneticists. Eugenics did not disappear. It renamed itself. What had thrived loudly in eugenics for decades quietly took postwar refuge under the labels of human genetics and genetic counseling."[11]

"In 1941, The American Breeders Association changed its name to the American Genetic Association and its publication from American Breeders Magazine to Journal of Heredity."[12]

The work could not be completed as DNA, it was not yet understood. Now it is understood and the temptation still exists.

Our culture has not changed in any significant way in the last fifty years. The impulses are the same and the possibility of creating the pure race is now within practical reach.

"The eugenics motto can be fulfilled. We must breed for quality, not quantity in the human species, or the end is nigh."[13]

How far will this culture go to control and maintain its perceived superiority? This culture drove the crusades initiated by Pope Urban I in the Thirteenth Century. The Quest inspired exploration of the world that resulted in the colonization of Africa, South and Central America and much of Asia.

Rudyard Kipling's poem, *The White Man's Burden* set the stage for the theoretical reason for expansion of the United States to the Pacific Ocean.

The White Man's Burden, 1899

Take up the White man's burden --
Send forth the best ye breed --
Go bind your sons to exile
To serve your captives' need;
To wait in heavy harness
On fluttered folk and wild --
Your new-caught, sullen peoples,
Half devil and half child.
Take up the White Man's burden --
In patience to abide,
To veil the threat of terror
And check the show of pride;
By open speech and simple,
An hundred times mad plain.
To seek another's profit,
And work another's gain.
Take up the White Man's burden --
The savage wars of peace --
Fill full the mouth of Famine
And bid the sickness cease;
And when your goal is nearest
The end for others sought,
Watch Sloth and heathen Folly
Bring all your hope to nought.
Take up the White Man's burden --
No tawdry rule of kings,
But toil of serf and sweeper --
The tale of common things.
The ports ye shall not enter,
The roads ye shall not tread,

Go make them with your living,
And mark them with your dead!
Take up the White man's burden --
And reap his old reward:
The blame of those ye better,
The hate of those ye guard --
The cry of hosts ye humour
(Ah, slowly!) toward the light: --
"Why brought ye us from bondage,
"Our loved Egyptian night?"
Take up the White Man's burden --
Ye dare not stoop to less --
Nor call too loud on freedom
To cloak your weariness;
By all ye cry or whisper,
By all ye leave or do,
The silent, sullen peoples
Shall weigh your Gods and you.
Take up the White Man's burden --
Have done with childish days --
The lightly proffered laurel,
The easy, ungrudged praise.
Comes now, to search your manhood
Through all the thankless years,
Cold-edged with dear-bought wisdom,
The judgment of your peers![14]

John L. O'Sullivan was the first to name an impulse that was present in Thomas Jefferson when he completed the Louisiana Purchase and presidents who followed him. The Monroe doctrine was the demand to the International Community to not interfere in the territorial expansion of the United States. The ideology was that the White people were destined by God to control the Western Hemisphere. O'Sullivan wrote, "The right of our manifest destiny to over spread and possess the whole of the continent, which

Providence has given us for the development of the great experiment of liberty a federative development of self government entrusted to us, is right such as that of the tree to the space of air and the earth suitable for the full expansion of its principle and destiny growth."[15]

The stage was set for the winning of the West. The expansion resulted in the near genocide of Native people and the destruction of their cultures. They needed to learn the correct way of living; their savage cultures had to be eradicated. It is after all the White man's burden. The opening of the West in the United States flew under the flag of manifest destiny. God wanted White civilization from sea to shining sea. Manifest Destiny is not even a thinly disguised cultural mandate. Again the conquest culture proceeded in the only way it knew. Providence ordained that it should be this way, the same way Merlin ordained the deeds of the Round Table.

This, however, is not manifested only in American History. The Voortrekkers marched into the center of South Africa and conquered the Zulu tribe and enslaved the Bantu people. They did so because they were mandated by God to take this land and civilize it. They too heard the call to accept the White Man's burden. The Zulu and Bantu suffered the same fate as the Native Americans.

There is a consistent pattern in it. We invaded Cuba in 1898 in response to an attack on the Lusitania. But, there was no attack on the Lusitania; the story was a fabrication so the United States could liberate Cuba. It happened again in Vietnam. My cousin, James Bond Stockdale, was the Naval Commander who led the attempt to defend against or find any Viet Cong attack boats. His mission was to verify a naval attack in the Gulf of Tonkin by the Viet Cong. When he returned to the Ticonderoga he was debriefed. "Did you see any boats? Not a one. No boats, no boat wakes, no ricochets off boats, no boat gunfire, no torpedo wakes – nothing but black sea and American firepower."[16] He was then shown the log of transmissions sent to Washington and the world. Toward the end of the transmission there was a remarkable series of statements doubting the truth of the earlier and perhaps staged transmission. "There were lines expressing doubt that there had been any boats out there that night at all."[17] The Pentagon and the president needed an attack and fabricated it. It was the reason for the bombing of Hanoi. The Gulf of Tonkin Resolution was the result.

This cultural myth story has clear self-identity and confidence. It is not a cultural myth story that is threatened when fun is poked at it. Miguel de Cervantes was perhaps the first to make fun of the story in *Don Quixote of the Mancha* published in 1605. Don Quixote is delusional. He has dreamed of being a Knight and finally dedicates himself to that role. He is Knighted in an inn/tavern that he thinks is a castle. His adventures are often misguided, resulting in unfortunate consequences. In Chapter 5 of *Don Quixote of the Mancha*, Cervantes carefully and deliberately connects Don Quixote as an extension of King Arthur and the Knights of the Round Table. The Broadway play, *The Man of La Mancha* features two songs, "*Climb Every Mountain*" and *"The Impossible Dream"* which embody many of the primary values of the Arthurian cultural myth. Even in the humor and the satire the cultural values are affirmed.

In a very similar way, Monty Python's film, *Search for the Holy Grail*, is a hilarious portrayal of the Arthur myth story. There is something of a cult following for this film. The culture feels no threat in the humor: the values are repeated and re-enforced.

While we can identify destructive outcomes of this culture we must acknowledge its strengths and gifts. The desire for the quest has made this an innovative and technological culture of genius. The quest in the areas of medicine, science, arts and technology has produced a profound and positive change in civilization.

It is innovative and adaptive. It arose in Sixth Century medieval Celtic Culture that would become England. It adapted itself to exploring the world and remade itself to be comfortable in the Old West and mining camps. The Arthur myth story can be set in science fiction and Western movies, or in a board room like Microsoft.

It is something of an unusual culture. It remains obscure for its members. It survives quite well in anonymity while it remains ever present through its myth story. When the stories of the myth are referenced, people recall many details and are often surprised they know the story so well.

The myth stories of most other cultures are caught in a particular time and setting which remain locked in the past. It is very difficult for these stories to adapt and move into the present and future. It is much more difficult for them to adapt to new contexts and realities.

While one could be pessimistic about ending racism in the Arthur culture, there is reason to be optimistic. The desire for the quest is the opportunity to invite this culture to a new place, an unexplored place that will carry great reward and peace. The quest to end racism and heal the racial relationships brings the promise that we can someday not be engaged in destructive and wasteful behavior. We can someday receive all of the gifts and abilities of people. Such gifts of culture and perspective can help us all find new meanings and new opportunities. We can be in relationship with people who are very different and learn from them and perhaps solve some of the riddles that continue to plague humanity. This may be the quest of the Holy Grail. The cup of the Last Supper is the cup of a new covenant, a new peace.

Admittedly, it is an improbable quest. We will need to give up power, control and privilege in this quest. The culture of Arthur has never been inclined to do so. In fact, the quest has always been about gaining power and control. Improbable as this quest may seem, the Arthur Culture does value justice and fairness. People are valued for what they do.

Camelot was at peace for forty years. Life was very good, filled with charm, adventure and hope. Perhaps our desire to find Camelot and return to it, is as near as repentance and reconciliation. The experience of the world is that African people would rather forgive than seek revenge. We all learned that in South Africa. If we apologize, repent and seek reconciliation perhaps our cultural myth will be fulfilled in its positive instead of acting out its negative form. Desmond Tutu's book, *No Future Without Forgiveness,* holds promise for us all.

It is time to proceed to the next task before us in this improbable quest. There is strong racist resistance to both Native Americans and African Americans. The persistent racism across the United States toward African Americans has continued even with direct effort to overcome and end it. What is it about African American Culture that is such a threat to the dominant culture?

CHAPTER FOUR

African American Culture

A Survival Culture

We must exercise great care when attempting to describe a culture other than our own. Imposition of our own cultural values will distort our view of the other culture. It may be this that has caused so many writers to describe African American culture as dysfunctional. It is, however, a strong, creative and vital culture that is no more dysfunctional than any other culture. With this caution in mind, I wish only to illustrate some of the marks of this culture and not offer a highly analytical or detailed description from a White perspective. The people most competent to complete that task are those who share that culture.

African American culture is fed by two streams. One stream is slavery and the other is African. These two streams created a Survival Culture that carries the scars of slavery and African values and traditions. The experience of slavery produced consequences that have continued to the present and by definition are counter to the dominant culture of the United States. The infrastructure of this culture is built in response to the experience of slavery.

The slave owner culture provided the foundation upon which slavery was practiced. The slaves survived by acting compliant while developing survival resources that were forbidden by the slave owner. Slave owners needed to destroy identity and culture of the African and any practice or tradition that would prevent this destruction had to be crushed. "The shrewd slave makers were fully aware that people who still respected themselves as human beings would resist to the death the dehumanizing process of slavery. Therefore, a systematic process of creating a sense of inferiority in the proud African was necessary in order to maintain them as slaves."[18] Meanwhile, Africans had to find ways to preserve identity through community and tradition. African culture provided this resource. The convergence of these two streams created a complex and strong culture, a culture that has survived consistent persecution and attack.

Any attempt to understand African American culture must recognize the scars and consequences of slavery. How did the slavery strategy work, and what was its process? We can find some important clues in a speech delivered by a White slave trader, William Lynch, on the bank of the James River in 1712. This well illustrates the strategy to control the slaves.

> *I have outlined a number of differences among the slaves; and I take these differences and make them bigger. I use fear, distrust and envy for control purposes. Take this simple little list of differences, and think about them. On the top of my list is "age," it is only there because it starts with "A." The second is "color" or shade. Then there is intelligence, size, sex, size of plantation, status on plantation, attitude of owners, whether the slaves live in the valley, on a hill, east, west, north, south, have fine or coarse hair or is tall or short. Now that you have list of differences, I shall give you an outline of action. You must pitch the old Black against the young Black. You must use*

the dark skin slaves against the light skin slaves and the light skin slaves against the dark skin slaves. You must also have your White servants and overseers distrust all Blacks. But it is necessary that your slaves trust and depend on us. They must love, respect and trust only us.

Gentlemen, these kits are your keys to control. Use them. Have your wives and children use them. Never miss an opportunity. My plan is guaranteed, and the good thing is that if used intensely for one year, the slaves themselves will remain perpetually distrustful.[19]

This speech points us to some issues that carry the marks of slavery in African American Culture.

The first problem the slave owner faced was one of control. These were proud and strong people who would resist being enslaved. A slave rebellion was a matter of life and death for the slave owner. The strength of the African was grudgingly respected and a strategy had to be developed. The first step was to define any and all differences between slaves and to use those differences to divide them and build distrust into them. They could never band together if they resented and mistrusted each other. Any sense of community on their part was very dangerous. On the one hand the slave owner saw the slaves as less than human, as cattle to be bred for profit and on the other hand they saw them as strong people whom they must crush.

The second problem facing the slave owner was to manipulate the slaves to trust only the slave owner. Slaves who have been effectively divided into competing groups may not be able to band together, but they still pose a serious threat to the slave owner. They may lose all sense of identity and be so disoriented that they may lash out as individuals and produce nothing of significant work. The new identity and loyalty must be attached to the slave owner. This is a more difficult task. Merciless treatment, whipping and beating can produce this through fear and intimidation. There is high cost however. Injured and battered slaves do not produce as much work. Happy slaves who feel content are more desirable. Children of slaves became very valuable. The ruthless intimidation became unnecessary in the second generation. The slave owner was able to control all factors in the children's lives. No parental authority, no practice of old traditions, no nurturing of identity was the best world for the slave owners. If culture gives us a sense of identity then how is identity formed in a culture born in slavery. "Many historians and slave narratives report how young children were separated from their mothers because the mother's love might cultivate some self respect in the child."[20]

The third problem faced by slave owners that we see reflected in this speech has to do with leadership. Slaves can never become leaders, as leaders can lead rebellions as well as workers. Overseers can never be allowed to bond with slaves at a personal level. Such relationships would develop sympathy on the part of the overseer and provide the seed bed for an alliance that the slave owner feared. The speech is clear. Be sure that the overseers never trust the slaves. The only person who can be trusted is the slave owner whom slaves rarely saw or encountered unless they worked in the house.

Disoriented Africans stolen from home, family and culture, transported in the holds of ships, dropped into an unknown place, brutalized and taught to fear the very people they might trust, could be totally controlled in a year. This is a remarkable statement. The fact it took that long is an affirmation of the strength and identity Africans brought with them.

Identity

The slave could never be allowed to have pride or a strong sense of identity. This would be a major undermining quality of the need for control. They could not have self respect for themselves or respect for each other. Family and culture provide identity and therefore both had to be disrupted. Mothers as we have already seen had to be separated from their children at birth. It was mothers who could impart feelings of value and purpose. Strong fathers who passed on the tradition and the life of being a man could never be allowed to interact with their children. Men were placed in the fields, or other labor separated from their children.

Remarkably this very thorough system of family and cultural disruption did not fully work. The slaves formed a culture among themselves that functioned as a secret society. They sang in code that the slave owner never decoded. These songs of hope, freedom and resistance were sung in the very presence the slave owners and overseers. Frederick Douglas in his book My Bondage, My Freedom describes his childhood being cared for by his grandmother. He knew his mother though he only met her once, and she knew him.

A Survival Culture was born in slavery. It did provide identity and values. The attempt to make sure the slaves did not trust each other did not work. They began to find ways to escape as did Frederick Douglass. Family patterns changed dramatically, but they did adapt to the harsh reality of slavery. Children were cared for and raised not on the basis of blood line, but on the basis of community. The Auntie child-raising system replaced the family patterns in Africa. Men were probably hunters and warriors in Africa and would have been the holders of the stories and traditions. They probably were less present in the child rearing process in Africa. The village would have been the child nurturing and raising setting in Africa. The absence of men in slavery would have left a huge gap, but one that could be filled by the Aunties.

"This dawning sense of people-hood was stimulated by external exigencies, by segregation on the plantation and in the towns, but it was stimulated also by internal exigencies, by the need to be together, by the need to express a different worldview, by the need to see beyond the blocked horizon." [20]

Community

As we can see, the attempt to crush community failed in some important ways. Community or perhaps communities did form in slavery. Child rearing adapted to this new context. However, the slave owner strategy did effectively divide slaves along artificial lines. Those lines were especially potent in regard to skin color and place of work. One of the most serious disturbances of community advancement coming from the slavery experience is disunity or "community division." The age-old pattern of divide-and-conquer was utilized along with so many other tricks in order to destroy African-American community life

Those who worked in the slave owner's house were perceived privileged by those who worked in the fields. Those with lighter skin were more likely to have less odious jobs. Those with lighter skin might even be able to pass and enter the White world. Lighter skin became prized but resented. The lighter skin of course was the result of White slave owners raping Black slaves. Out of that violence came the lighter skin that was seen as privileged as opposed to darker skin. The definition of being African became a point of contention. This division is still a reality and provides the continuing opportunity to divide the African American community. We can only affirm that this is a consequence of slavery and illustrates the unfinished business of slavery. The White community must not only own this reality but must recognize the ways in which we exploit it. "This sense of inferiority still affects us in many ways. Our inability to respect African-American leadership, our persistent and futile efforts to look like and act like Caucasian people, is based upon this sense of inferiority. The persistent tendency to think of dark skin as unattractive, kinky hair as 'bad' hair, and African features as less appealing than Caucasian features, come from this sense of inferiority."[21]

We could describe this culture as being a community culture, which would suggest that it is the same as the Conquest Culture. This would be a gross misunderstanding. This culture is not a familial culture in a classic sense either. It is founded in family relationships but welcomes and includes friends who are outside the family. Sometimes this even includes Northern Europeans. This culture is uncommon in this regard. The Conquest Culture is a community culture, but it is a community of individuals. The Survival Culture is a community culture of families. This is but one example of the subtle yet substantive differences. It is this difference that results in totally different world-views and values between these two cultures. They not only see the world differently, they view events, history, values and truth virtually from diametrically opposed positions.

Leadership

"Every leader or scholar who has attempted to address African-American community problems poses this destructive disunity as the most deadly disease in our communities."[22] Again we see the consequence of slavery. Leadership was so manipulative and divisive by design this new culture at its birth distrusted leadership. There have been many strong and powerful leaders in the African American community, but each has been neutralized by this distrust. Bringing this whole community together will require overcoming the consequences of slavery. Martin Luther King, Jr. did seem to be able to do that at least for a period of time.

This problem plays a major role in the relationship to the culture of the United States. African American culture is placed at an immediate disadvantage in that the culture of King Arthur idolizes strong leaders and sees weakness as the absence of strong leadership. This disadvantage is often exploited as White culture easily is able to undermine emerging strong leaders in the African American community.

Work/Achievement

Perhaps the most potent consequence of slavery is the perception of work and achievement that results. "Work was not fulfilling or valued; work was completed to avoid something more painful. Work was drudgery and was resented. The work only benefited the slave owner who did not care what happened to the person performing the work."[23] This emerging culture obviously would not value work or achievement. What was there to be achieved? Perhaps one could get back to the slave quarters without being whipped or threatened, or worse, at the end of the day. The greatest achievement was to get some bad food and a night's sleep on a bad bed. The next morning one did it all over again. The slave owned nothing; anything the slave had belonged to the slave owner including their own lives. There was nothing one could do to get something for the work, nothing would make life better, and it was what it was. Work only benefited the White community; work was for the benefit of others. This cultural reality does connect in a profoundly negative way to the White culture and functions as a self-fulfilling prophecy in regard to racist stereotypes.

Resistance

Slaves had to at least appear to comply. Non compliance resulted in severe punishment. Resistance to slavery however, was obvious as has been stated earlier. The feelings and resentments had to be stuffed down and contained. There are those who affirm that this pattern continues to create health problems in African Americans: such as hypertension, high blood pressure, heart disease and depression. This resistance and the anger that goes with it have boiled over from time to time, always at the expense of the African American.

The resistance is felt and known, however. Anyone who interacts with African Americans recognizes strength, talent and ability. They seem determined in their refusal to accept or assimilate into White culture. There have been a number of public voices that have been very forceful in declaring this refusal. Malcolm X and The Black Power Movement are two examples. White culture assumes that they are either resistant, revolutionary, or stupid. Nothing ever was nor now is as frightening in the slave owner as a revolutionary. The alternate choice is more comfortable, they must be stupid. If conversation between White and Black ever gets past the simple polite level, the anger becomes apparent. This anger triggers the denial of White culture and is often greeted by the response that African Americans need to get over it and quit whining. The cultural clashes are constant and devastating to relationship building.

This reality is exacerbated by the fact that African Americans are caught in a bicultural disconnect. On the one hand White people assume that African Americans have no culture other than the White culture. After all, they have been in the midst of this culture for a very long time. They know how our culture works, they live in it, they earn a living in it and they raise their children in it. White society thinks this means that they share our culture. Actually, they have learned to live in our culture while remaining apart from it. Many African Americans continue to affirm that they are not of our culture and do not wish to be, and in fact refuse to be. To become part of the culture that enslaved ancestors, and continues to carry racist attitudes against them is nonsensical. As a result affirmation of their culture is problematic as the consequences of slavery continue to be played out.

The slavery stream developed a strong and adaptive culture that learned how to survive in the most adverse of conditions. It strikes me as odd that many White observers see this culture as flawed and even pathological due to its place of birth. It seems to me that its place of birth has provided the primary cultural values and skills to continue to survive in an adverse setting. This is not weakness it is strength.

The African Stream

In the early 1990s we took a group of White middle class high school youth to Cameroon. Our purpose was to introduce these White students to another world, another culture and help them learn that they were not the center of the universe. Our youth teamed with Bulu young people to provide a two week conference for young people in the villages that surround Metet, Cameroon.

Our arrival was a powerful moment. When we were yet about a quarter mile from Metet we saw women dressed in white on both sides of the road. When they saw our bus, they began singing and playing drums. They were waving what looked like small palm branches. The bus slowed and they continued to sing and welcome us. As we arrived at Metet they surrounded us and took us to a large lawn area. All the while they were singing and shouting "Welcome". They identified me as the leader and led me to a wicker lounge chair with a very high back on it. It became obvious this simple wicker chair symbolized a throne for them. If a throne could be made out of wicker this was it. They brought water, fruit and juice. Our group was seated in a half circle; the rest of the circle was completed by Bulu parents and young people. The music began again. They performed a small play with children dressed in costumes. It was rather elaborate and filled with song, humor and great energy. The play welcomed us and introduced us to some of the stories that explained who they were and why they cared for us. It was very moving. Those American young people talked about that experience for the next several years. For all of us this was our first time in Africa. We had just received our first lesson in the ways of Africa and the remarkable cultures that reside there.

About five years later we returned to Africa, this time to South Africa. We were visiting with people about the process of ending Apartheid, the Truth and Reconciliation Commission and observing the terrible consequences of government run racism. We visited a church in the Black township of Alexandra on Easter Sunday. Maake Masango was the pastor, and still is. Again, we received a stunning welcome in that township. After worship we went to one of the member's home for a meal provided by people of meager means. They welcomed us with song and lighthearted energy. It struck us as amazing that these people who had been so brutalized by White people were so welcoming to White people. We did not see resentment or anger in them; we received warmth and friendship.

In 2004 we returned to South Africa. This time we traveled with a group that was half African American and half White. Two particular events were striking. First, the children of the townships, which are still in massive poverty, were not in the least bit frightened by White people. The older youth would have experienced White apartheid police raids in their townships, but they received us with warmth and friendship. Adults were willing and able to speak candidly with us about their situation, their hopes, their dreams and their resentments.

During both trips to South Africa, we were struck by the open discussion of racism, naming it and resolving to end it. They spoke to us from identity that was intact and clear. The culture was alive and well. Apartheid had not destroyed it. In our first trip, a woman at the Alexandra church told me the apartheid police had shot and killed her two children. Her story of that event was devastating. She concluded by saying that she would never forget but had forgiven those who had killed her children. Over and over again we heard the affirmation that this brutality must stop and therefore they would not take revenge or continue to hate. Revenge and hate would only cause it to happen again.

While in South Africa in 2004 we experienced a second powerful moment. Our African American friends were invited to go to the front of the church at the end of the service. The congregation welcomed them back to Africa and chose an African name for each one. This was a very powerful moment for us all. That act was a fulfillment and a confirmation of their feelings about being in Africa. It was home for them. They understood it and identified the customs, dance and traditions that they continue to practice in the United States. The cultural bond was very strong and the African Americans and the Black South Africans knew it intuitively.

African Americans commented that their experience was both exciting and frustrating. They saw Black South Africans living with the consequences of slavery, yet they knew who they were. Their identity was clear and forceful. They talked freely and celebrated freely and welcomed freely. The African Americans talked a lot about wishing they had the same thing. They wished that they knew as clearly their identity. Many described that lack as a hole in their lives and were excited and saddened to see what they had missed.

African culture survived slavery. New slaves kept arriving bringing culture with them and the slave culture kept hanging on to traditions and values. Of course this became only partial and probably fragmented. The issue of identity was exactly the point of attack by slave owners. The new slave culture incorporated values, traditions, music and stories. It was African culture that held those slaves together and provided the tools to survive.

It is visible even to a White person. I have seen the welcome in Metet in the United States; I have seen it in communities, groups and churches. I have seen welcome even of those who perpetrated hatred, not in a sentimental way, but in a real way, offering forgiveness following accountability. I have heard the music, seen the dance and experienced the strength. I am not an anthropologist who can chart and describe every custom, tradition and song to its point of origin. That is not the point. The point is that this culture called African American has been informed by and formed in an African context. What makes this amazing is the African context was not in Africa but on plantations in the United States that practiced brutal and oppressive slavery. This African context existed in the very presence of those who sought to destroy it and crush the identity of all who were part of it. In that African context was forged a new culture, and like all cultures it had flaws and difficulties. This new culture survived slavery, the brutality of the reconstruction era, Jim Crow laws, segregation and an ongoing racism that continues to denigrate and dismiss it.

This is a culture of great strength and versatility. This culture has produced many outstanding people and made huge contributions to the culture and society of the United States. Though most of those contributions have not been acknowledged, they continue to be made. As African Americans continue to learn of their own history and are able to tell the heroic stories of their culture, perhaps their sense of lost identity will be healed.

We need to read and study their history. We need to learn the names of the heroes, leaders, scientists, teachers, doctors and others who have made contributions to our well being as a nation. We need to sit with African Americans in our communities and hear their stories. We will meet more heroes and leaders as we do so. This is an easy treasure hunt for us. The gifts and abilities are abundant and they are waiting for us to see them. We have looked many times before, but have failed to see. We need to see.

CHAPTER FIVE

Conquest versus Survival

Racism as Consequence of Cultural Clash

White Culture and African American culture stand face to face and represent the most difficult conflict to resolve. It is a values conflict. The conflict is between a conquest culture and a survival culture. The goals of these two cultures are at cross purposes. The conquest culture expects and desires to conquer the other culture and assimilate that culture into itself. The conquest culture is convinced that it knows best for everyone and expects that others will recognize that fact. Resistance to that purpose is frustrating to the conquest culture and the effort to conquer is intensified. Cultures that have been able to resist this pressure are few and those that do become an isolated globe.

Survival cultures strongly resist being co-opted. The culture is the vehicle of survival as it provides identity and values. For African American culture resistance is filled with the consequences of slavery and all that has happened since. The White culture is the slave owner culture, it is the culture of segregation and Jim Crow laws, and it is the culture that has refused to provide access and opportunity for African Americans. To become a part of that culture is to sell out and betray all of those who have suffered in the past. This is not an option. Even if the two cultures were compatible it is unlikely that assimilation would take place. "African American culture holds a world view that carries the ethos of Africa. The cultural values associated with this worldview are, cooperation, interdependence, and collective responsibility. The Euro-American emphasizes the survival of the fittest and control over nature. The cultural values associated with this world view are competition, individualism and independence." [24] In order to examine this conflict and recognize it as the source of and energy for racism we need to compare and contrast the two cultures at five key points: resistance, leadership, identity, role of males in the family, and work/achievement.

Resistance

The culture of King Arthur wants to help people by giving them a better life and teaching them how to achieve. There is earnest desire to overcome evil and to rescue those caught in evil. We want to be the white knight saving the world. This conviction rests on the assumption that no one else has ever gotten it right and it is unlikely they ever will if we do not help them and instruct them. Certainly, they will appreciate our efforts because we want them to be like us and succeed like we have. We are the wealthiest nation in the world because we have the correct answers and methods. As I have traveled in underdeveloped nations, many times I have heard White Americans marvel at how happy the people are and yet live in poverty. It is a telling cultural comment.

White culture will analyze the changes that need to be made in order to achieve success. Whites believe the Latinos are losing very productive work and enterprise time by taking a siesta every afternoon. They have a very large noon meal, sleep and then go back to work until eight or nine. This disrupts the business day and wastes time and productivity. Opening and closing a business twice a day is not efficient. Latinos respond "This time in the middle of the day is necessary and essential. It is the gathering time for the whole family. This is time that is too valuable to use running a business. Family is crucial to all of life and business must work around it. Money is not that important; we are living comfortably and are happy to leave it there."

To the ears of the White culture this means they have their priorities backwards, and they will never succeed. They are lazy; they'd rather nap than work. Time is not important to them and until it is they will never succeed in business. They would rather sit under a tree sleeping with their sombreros over their faces. They are too slow, not prompt and simply not aggressive enough to succeed.

This disdain for Latinos is a caricature built on stereotypes that are the bedrock of racism. They resist our help, they are either lazy or stupid or both. They don't have anything we want so we will ignore them and maybe someday they will wake up.

In the Latino case it is simply a matter of not accepting our advice. For African Americans however, the problem is much bigger. They live in this country. They should know how it works. They have been told to work hard and yet they don't. They should know this is true; the evidence is all around them on a daily basis.

The resistance is persistent and vocal. Day in and day out they are confronted by racism and told to work harder. Resistance is filled with frustration and anger. If they try to share their feelings they are dismissed and told to stop playing the victim. If their anger spills out they will be put down and even ridiculed. The anger sounds like resistance and defensiveness.

This apparent resistance is threatening and fear producing in the White community. The Black Power movement was frightening to White culture because it proposed to take power and not remain submissive to it. "Black is Beautiful" sounded like Black Nationalism. I remember hearing White people say, "These people don't want to learn the right way to do anything, they are just a mob. They don't want to work for anything they just want to take it. They want to tear this perfect union apart and destroy all that is good. We cannot let them do it; their stupidity cannot be our undoing. If they move into the neighborhood then these ignorant and uncivilized people will destroy what we have worked so hard to maintain. The police need to stop them when they are in a White neighborhood because they are probably up to no good. They are always looking for the easy way out; that's why they are criminals and drug pushers. Some of them are okay, but most of them are just ignorant and dangerous people. I have nothing against Black people; some of them are my best friends."

This sequence of racist responses is all fueled by the resistance that African Americans have toward assimilation by the White culture. In the final analysis it is all wrapped in the denial of racism, the White person is describing what they see as fact. "Truth will never be validated by ignorance or denial. Sometimes truth is easily recognizable and other times you have to dig deep to uncover it. You'll never find truth if you are afraid of the dark, afraid to search the thoughts in the inner recesses of your mind."[25] This conflict point may be central to the ongoing racism in the United States. Refusal to assimilate is the single most offensive idea that White culture can imagine. We can see the differences of these two cultures and the resulting clash as we recall the functions of culture.

Identity

Culture provides identity. We are named as a group. Our history gives us stories of heroes and courageous events.

Our culture gives us a belonging and pride in who we are. The stories and heroes are clear in White culture. We have accounts of victory over evil, stories of conquests and endurance through long hardship. We know who we are and not uncommonly get a bit extreme about it all. We can go anywhere we wish to go at any time. A person of average means can walk into any five-star hotel or restaurant and be welcomed easily. That welcome will end only if they are unable to pay the bill. We can buy a home, get a job, enroll our children in schools and can probably afford to pay for most of it. We can drive through an exclusive neighborhood at night and not be noticed. It is White privilege. In White culture people can predict with great accuracy how they will be received wherever they go. There are very few settings that a White person wouldn't feel comfortable entering regardless of means or status. Identity is both cultural and personal. Knowing who you are personally is as valued as knowing who you are culturally. Determining one's identity and following it is the final stage of maturing in White culture. Identity informs vocational choice, lifestyle and primary life goals. It is expected that these issues are resolved by the time a person is in their mid 20s. Individuals who remain largely dependent on parents or live at home at this point are held in some suspicion.

The rebellion against cultural norms that often takes place in the late teens and into college is generally tolerated. This is considered a phase or process to establish individuality. It is expected that the rebellious young person will be a pillar of the culture later in their life. Many of those who went to extreme rebellion in the 1960s and 70s are now fully in the mainstream. Woodstock is an event that many went to and now brag about, but few of them would go if it happened now. They would be out of place with their $500 suits and BMWs.

The very source of confidence in the White community is a matter of great difficulty in the African American community. There is a bicultural disconnect in the African American experience. African Americans are in White culture but not of it. They have learned how to act in the White context. They know the work and social protocols, none of which are intuitive for them. They are African but not fully African. They are drawn to Africa and feel at home in Africa but experience great loss of what has been denied them by slavery. They see Africans with strong identity and community and wish it was theirs. They see people who know their past, their traditions and culture, and wish they knew those same things. In many respects African Americans struggle to find a cultural home. It certainly is not White culture and they can only wish to be part of African culture.

This creates immense ambiguity for both African Americans and White Americans. Again to White ears this ambiguity sounds like adolescent rebellion. Failure to follow the identity and career regimen of White young people suggests that there is something wrong with African American young people. "Why can't they just settle in, go to college, get a good job and become part of the mainstream?" Few White Americans are bicultural and have little experience to draw upon. As a result there is limited acknowledgement of this ambiguity that is so complex for African Americans.

When African American young people attempt to establish an identity that is African the response is often ridicule. "They have never been to Africa. They have been raised here and educated here. Who are they kidding?" If, an African American youth overtly attempts to fit into White American identity, he/she will likely be ridiculed by peers and friends. The Oreo or Uncle Tom labels are always lurking nearby.

This is compounded by the unwillingness to consider the long term consequences of slavery. The mere suggestion that slavery has something to do with current life often brings the White response: "I had nothing to do with slavery. Slavery happened a long time ago; no one living today was ever a slave or slave owner. They need to take responsibility and quit using slavery as an excuse." This response refuses to acknowledge that African American culture learned to survive in slavery by building strong defenses. Values, family issues and identity were formed in that context. In just a short and quick review, we have seen the powerful impact slavery had in the formation of this culture.

Attempts by African Americans to discuss the consequences of slavery or reparation are met with the accusation of using the "race card." Many Whites see this as "the trump card" which is used to make us feel guilty and open us to manipulation. The offense of the race card is that it confronts our denial and forces us to see what we do not want to see. How do we defend ourselves from this strategy by African Americans? It's rather simple: we dismiss it one more time as the whining of a group who love being victims. The integrity of African Americans is challenged and maligned. "Black people just make stuff up to get special privilege. Black people are low performing whiners; you can't believe anything they say."

This is a major hurdle in Black/White relationships. Blacks cannot tell White people how they really feel or what has happened to them in the past. Blacks try to report experiences of racism and are discounted as reliable reporters, when people are presented with information that conflicts with their belief system. I have come to expect three basic reactions:

1. They will reject all of the information, often before considering it.

2. They will sift through the information and embrace that with which they are most comfortable.

3. They will consider all of the facts with an open mind and accept the conclusions they reach."[26]

What is factual? The O.J. Simpson trial should have been a learning moment for us all. Culture determines how we see and understand the information that constantly swirls around us. Fact for one culture is nonsense to another. It's not just about data; it is also about feelings, hurts and experiences. White people must learn that Blacks are reliable and valid witnesses, who have genuine feelings and hurts. We must learn to listen, and not dismiss what we hear to preserve our own security and denial. Identity issues are another source of racism that arises out of our cultural conflict.

Leadership

Not surprisingly, leadership is highly esteemed in White culture. The Knights of the Round Table were all leaders. They were expected to go on quests to lead people out of evil, conquer the evil, find the treasure, or whatever. To seek leadership and the esteem that accompanies it is a common goal in White culture. We hold leaders to a higher standard of behavior and practice. It is not uncommon that violation of those standards results in exile from the leadership world. The length of exile depends upon the perceived type or degree of violation. Some leaders can find their way back but many do not. Political figures like Spiro Agnew, Richard Nixon and Gary Hart were never able to return to leadership positions. Bill Clinton, on the other hand, has maintained leadership, though not in elected office. The same applies to sports figures. Pete Rose violated a foundational rule and has not been admitted to the Hall of Fame though his credentials meet the qualifications. It is also true that there is a long trail of sports figures that have passed in and out of the judicial system with only minor short term sanctions.

White culture often lionizes leaders of the past. Heroic qualities are ascribed to them. These leaders may face controversy and difficulty but ultimately are seen as great people. Winston Churchill was voted out as Prime Minister as a failure only to return and lead England through World War II. He is now a giant of history. While leaders do not always succeed at maintaining the standards, the culture continues to hope one of them will be a new King Arthur.

Every presidential election has this undercurrent. We look for the perfect, ideal leader to be president. Within 90 days of the inauguration the hope begins to dim. John Kennedy was the most successful President in this endeavor. The White House was portrayed as Camelot. The family relationships were idyllic. They were all very attractive and appealing. He even led a nationwide quest to land a man on the moon.

Marketing and image making have become ever more crucial tasks in election campaigns. An appealing image must be created and anything that might be appealing in the opponent must be destroyed.

Slaves were never allowed leadership roles. The only voice of leadership came from the slave owner. Slaves were manipulated by exploiting physical differences. Light skinned slaves worked in the slave owner's house while darker skinned worked in the fields. Every possible device was used to pit slave against slave. Any sign of leadership by slaves of other slaves was immediately punished.

These internal divisions persist in the African American community. Leadership is not trusted. The cultural underlying assumption is that leaders are the tools of the slave owner, or they represent one group against the other. The community division that was deliberately practiced by slave owners has left continuing division in the African American Culture. This outcome of slavery has seriously crippled the ability of leaders to draw the community together and achieve consensus.

Strong Black leadership will always make White people nervous. What could really happen if a strong Black leader organized and was supported by a vast majority Black people? Martin Luther King, Jr. did that and was immediately under investigation by the FBI. Why the investigation? White people learned long ago that if some negative information can be found regarding a Black leader, then that Black leader would be neutralized in the White community while driving a wedge in the Black community. Negative voices were starting to be raised in the Black community before the assassination of Martin Luther King. Some insisted that nonviolence was not effective and that King was slowing the progress of equal rights. Others were concerned about his early attacks on the War in Vietnam. Eldridge Cleaver, Malcolm X, Louis Farrakhan and others have been strong voices heard as extreme in the White community. At the same time, they have apparently been unable to rally the majority of the Black community.

The case of O. J. Simpson illustrates the division between White and Black perceptions of leadership and success. The White community tended to believe that O. J. got off because he was wealthy and had expensive attorneys. In this perspective O. J. was guilty as charged. The Black community saw O. J. as a successful Black man who threatened the stereotypes of White culture. "O. J. is another example of the White power structure wanting to knock down the successful Black man. O. J. in this perspective was an innocent victim of the Los Angeles police."

The discounting of African American leadership coupled with the discounting of African American integrity provides yet another cultural tag point for racism. Black leaders are easily put down and ridiculed by the White media because it is unlikely there will be a unified community to defend that leader. The failure to take Black leadership seriously allows the White community to offer the racist conclusion that Blacks lack this ability. They are not adequate leaders because they are Black. Paradoxically, Martin Luther King's "*I Have a Dream*" speech has become an icon in the United States. Given enough time, a highly talented and gifted Black leader can receive grudging respect and honor. White people can now say, "He was right, and those unfortunate things like segregation are over now. We are past that all now. There is a National Holiday celebrating him and we will hear his speech again. It is a great day for the Black Community. Racism is over, isn't it?"

Work/Achievement

For African American culture work is for the benefit of someone else. Work is drudgery that carries no benefit for the person doing the work. The benefit is only for the White that owns the work done. White culture values work as the primary tool for wealth and achievement. When a culture does not value work and material benefit, White culture concludes they are lazy and lack initiative. These two contrasting worldviews, one of cooperation, the other competition is another cultural conflict. Work in the African American worldview is a group effort for the community, while in White culture work is individual for the benefit of the individual. Work done in the White context by an African American brings these two worldviews into direct conflict. In addition, in the White context the control of the work removes interdependence and establishes dependence.

When we took a group of high school youth to Cameroon they planned a youth conference with Bulu youth. Teams of six, three American and three Bulu, were formed to plan and prepare for the conference.

I watched one of these groups for about an hour one morning. Their assignment was to dig six holes for poles for a power line. The holes had to be about four feet deep. The soil was not hard to dig and the work seemed easy to accomplish in a few hours. The six all showed up at the proper place at the proper time but there was only one shovel. The Americans wanted to get started immediately and get the work done. They had ideas about how to dig the holes, ways to measure the depth and the necessary size of the circumference of each hole. They also thought it would be best if each person dug one hole. A long conversation began in English, French and Bulu.

The Bulus thought it better to dig the holes together, one person with the shovel and the others pulling dirt out of the hole with their hands. Somehow unclear to me, all finally agreed to the Bulu method. The first person with the shovel was a Bulu who leaned on the shovel as they all talked. The continued combination of hand gestures and charades was puzzling. They seemed to have arrived at a conclusion but nothing was happening, just more conversation.

Finally, the Bulu young man began to dig but the conversation continued. This meant that digging had to stop to accommodate the hand gestures. About two hours after they began, the first hole was dug. The Americans were ready to move to the second hole. The Bulus were not. They sat around the hole and talked some more. I met the pastor of the Bulu Church and asked him about this. He spoke English very well so we were able to avoid the hand gestures. He explained to me that for Bulus work is an occasion to share socially. For Bulus digging the hole was secondary. I told him for Americans the exact opposite was true. The task of digging the hole was the priority, social exchange was secondary. He smiled and said, "What a wonderful opportunity for both Americans and Bulus to dig a hole together." He was right.

That evening I talked with the Americans who had been part of that group. They needed serious debriefing. They were frustrated and upset because it had taken all day to dig three holes. We talked a long time and finally they agreed to keep working at it. Without that conversation they would have concluded that Bulus are lazy and can't get anything done. There is a similar clash about work between White Americans and African Americans.

This same difference in worldview informs assumptions about education. Educational assumptions are driven by the culture in which they reside. Northern Europeans assume that cognitive processes are the same for everyone. Our assumptions are that the highest value lies in the object or in the acquisition of the object. We know best through defining, counting and measuring. We look for the right answer empirically, which often leads us to the dichotomy of either/or.

"African, Hispanic and Native American cultures see the highest value in interpersonal relationships and one knows through symbolic imagery and opposites are united as both/and."[27] *This creates a more abrasive cultural clash in a society that increasingly values technology over relationships and has a strong tendency to define issues as either/or. "The educational system as it has developed both in Europe and America is an antiquated process, which*

does not hit the mark even in the case of the needs of the White man himself. If the White man wants to hold on to it, let him do so; but the Negro, so far as he is able, should develop and carry out a program of his own. The philosophy and ethics resulting from our educational system have justified slavery, peonage, segregation, and lynching."[28]

Student achievement and success in education certainly are greatly affected by the worldview of the educational program when an alternate worldview is held by the student. The White response has insisted that our way is the right way and they need to learn by this method and this worldview; they must adjust. To date the adjustment does not seem to be taking place. These two worldviews are in daily conflict in the schools of the United States.

This clash begins with the cultural assumptions of a world view. The White racism sees inferiority and underachievement as another example of the inadequacy of African Americans. In the case of our educational systems, racism becomes a self fulfilling prophesy.

Two strong and very different cultures stand face to face and neither will be moved. The chasm between them grows as the conflict confirms the racism of the White culture and builds the anger and resentment of African Americans. The more resentment on the one side, the more predictable is the racism on the other. The chasm continues to widen.

Let's be clear about our participation in all of this. In my experience most White people would affirm to create systems that predetermine the failure of any particular group. Most White people probably want everyone to have a fair share of the pie, but the pie is a finite amount. The pie has already been allocated with the largest portion going to White people. The pie must be bigger before redistribution is possible; we don't want to give our portion of the pie away; others must earn a bigger portion or provide more pie. The fact is that the system makes this virtually impossible. This is the pain being suffered by White South Africans following Apartheid and as expected they are resentful.

The racism is real, but it is unintentional and cannot be fixed by passing new societal laws. Racism is born in the clash between a Conquest Culture and Survival Culture. We cannot readily, if ever, change these two cultures. We need to find a way to live together in the midst of the clash between these two cultures. Until we can do that racism will continue to be an ever widening chasm. We must begin exploring how we undo racism when we realize and understand that it is born and nurtured in the clash between two very strong cultures.

CHAPTER SIX

Madrona: The Way Racism Works

This was to be a routine visit. The pastor of Madrona Presbyterian Church in Seattle had retired. How did the elected leaders, the session, wish to proceed? There were a variety of options for pastoral leadership. Ivan, the Committee on Ministry Chair, and I were there to review those options. This was a routine step in the process of securing a new pastor.

We knew most of the session and other members of the church in attendance at the meeting. Some of them I knew very well. Daisy Dawson had been a member and the chair of the Personnel Committee, which reviewed and evaluated my work. I had worked closely with her in some difficult employee terminations. Gladys Edelton had been staff to a close colleague and long time friend. The Rosses were long time members and had served on various Presbytery committees. This was a not a group of strangers.

Daisy Dawson had accomplished much in her life. She was experienced and had great insight. I liked and respected her. She had a great sense of humor and a warm caring personality. She had been a member, elder and leader in Madrona since the 1940s, as had Gladys and the Rosses.

This African American congregation included a number of White and some younger members. It was a small congregation and was struggling financially. They had, however, put in an elevator and improved the entrance to the building a few years earlier. They could not afford a full time pastor, but the previous half-time pastor had worked well with them and we expected that would be the case with a new pastor.

We had talked about finding an African American pastor who might help them focus their identity, but that decision would be theirs to make. This was not a congregation embroiled in conflict nor was it a congregation that faced any great crisis. Our visit was routine; we had nothing unusual to propose. They needed to review their options to make a decision that would start the process.

When Ivan and I entered the fellowship hall there were about 25 people present. This was unusual. We had indicated that deacons and members of the church would be welcome if they wanted to attend the meeting. In most situations only the session attends and not always all of them. They greeted us warmly as usual and we got underway. We outlined the various options for pastoral leadership and suggested that the young African American who had been working with the youth could be commissioned as Lay Pastor and he might be an option. This would require that while serving them he would enter seminary.

There was some unusual edginess among them that morning. There was a tension in the room. There was some bickering between elders and members as we reviewed the various options for securing a pastor... At first it appeared to be nothing more than the usual anxiety created by the departure of a beloved pastor. The questions became more pointed. How would potential candidates be found? Who would do the search? "It depends upon the option you choose," we said. In some cases we would propose names, in some options they would do a full search and if they liked the Commissioned Lay Pastor option the search was already completed. What criteria would we use if we suggested names? How would we control a full search if they chose that option? The word 'control' seemed to be a code word for them. We told them that we would check references of candidates they might choose and if a problem emerged we might not approve a candidate. This answer, though routine for Ivan and I, was not routine for them. The agitation level increased dramatically.

A most surprising and stunning statement soon followed. The surprise was who spoke and what she said was quite stunning. Daisy Dawson leaned across the table pointing at me. Her eyes danced with anger and her voice had a firm and accusatory tone. She said, "You have been trying to close this church for 40 years and we are not going anywhere, you aren't going to do it." Such an idea was never on our agenda but obviously there was no reason to dispute her. This was a conviction of a leader of the church for whom I had much respect. I was overwhelmed and speechless. Voices in the room agreed and heads were nodding.

It required little perceptive ability to know something was going on here that neither Ivan nor I understood... I had been in Seattle for about five years and had never heard anyone suggest that Madrona should be closed, but everyone in that room agreed with Daisy. Some other people commented that Madrona had had pastors forced on them in the past and they were tired of that as well.

Obviously Ivan and I had misunderstood the purpose of this meeting. Somehow we needed to understand what lay behind the anger we had just witnessed. We asked them if they would be willing to return the next Saturday and tell us their story. We could spend as much time as it took on that day. There was some reticence on their part, but they finally agreed on the basis that they didn't have much to lose. Some expressed doubt that it would make any difference. We left feeling that we had taken a number of direct hits that morning and weren't sure what we would hear the next week, but we had to learn this information in order to help them find a new pastor.

We must be very clear in understanding what happened. Ivan and I did very little in this process. We agreed to listen to their story. They were the ones who were being asked to do the hard work and would take all of the risks. As they indicated, they had raised these issues before and were ignored or worse were accused of lying. Why would they think it would be different this time? While they hesitated, they did decide to risk it one more time. Perhaps Ivan and I were a little safer as we knew nothing of this story before that morning. The tension in the meeting was the result of previous experiences. By their account they were expecting to be told who their next pastor would be. They were upset by this possibility as the meeting was convened.

The next Saturday the tension was still in the room, but it was different. This was nervous tension; they were anxious though still warm in their welcome to us. It took a while for people to begin talking. We had told them that we would listen to their story and we were willing to be there as long as it took. They began by giving us some background information. I suspect this seemed safe to them as they tested our willingness to listen.

Many of them were raised as Presbyterians and had graduated from Presbyterian colleges. Many of them had their roots in the Southeastern United States. They understood the Presbyterian Church and were intensely loyal to it. They reminded us of their role in the Presbytery and the leadership they had provided. We affirmed that fact and thanked them for their leadership. Finally, the story began to be told. They began by telling us that in 1953 the Presbytery had decided to merge Grace Presbyterian Church, which was African American, with Madrona Presbyterian, a White church. White members of the Presbytery who remembered the event also said the two churches were merged. When we read the minutes of the Presbytery meetings in which the decision was made we found incongruity. There was no merger agreement, no merger plan nor any action reflecting a merger. Grace was closed and members were encouraged to attend the church of their choice. The real property, the building and its contents were sold.

The intention driving the decision was apparently in response to desegregation and the work of Dr. Martin Luther King. The church should not be segregated and these two congregations were not far apart. However, again those minutes do not reflect any process of preparation for the two congregations. Grace was closed and Madrona was the nearest congregation, so the deal was done.

The Black folks were somewhat reluctant because they were not sure how they would be received. How would they be able to take their traditions and perspective into a White church? To relieve their fears, a series of promises were made to them. First, their pastor, Ray Day, would go with them to Madrona. He would be one of the pastors of the "merged" new church. He was African American and deeply loved by the congregation. Second, the Grace building would be sold and the proceeds would resolve a number of problems in the Madrona building. The roof needed to be replaced; it had leaked badly and the interior plaster was in very bad repair. The building needed painting on the outside, and the furnace needed to be replaced. The cost of all this work would exceed the sale price of the Grace Church property. They were assured that additional funds from the Presbytery would be applied to complete all of the repairs.

On Easter Sunday, they met at Grace Church for the last time and walked to the Madrona building. They were deeply saddened and apprehensive. Everyone was celebrating Easter except them; this was a sad day. When they arrived for worship several had their choir robes with them. They asked where the choir was meeting so they could join. They were told that they were not welcome in the choir; Black faces in front of their church every Sunday was not acceptable to this White church. The devastation had only begun.

Grace Church was sold for $6,500. The Presbytery action indicated that these funds would be used for Madrona and the new church on Mercer Island. Mercer Island had never been part of the conversation with the people from Grace. The first thing the Presbytery did was pay off a loan to the General Assembly in the amount of $1,500. No one at Grace had ever heard anything of that transaction. The roof was patched but continued to leak, the furnace was repaired and a garage was painted. The balance of the sale money was about $1,000. There is no report of the proceeds from the sale of the contents of the Grace building. This plus the thousand dollars was never accounted for, but most likely was used in the development process of the new church on Mercer Island. The additional funds that were promised never were given. The Madrona building remained in bad repair and while $120,000 was being spent on Mercer Island; no additional funds were provided to Madrona except a loan 10 years later to replace the roof.

The most devastating experience for them, however, was the announcement that Ray Day would not be a pastor in Madrona. Their worst fears had come to pass. The experiences on that very first Sunday confirmed their fear, and Ray Day would not be there to speak for them.

White flight began and many Whites left the church. Many of the Grace people left for other African American churches. The neighborhood changed and became predominantly Black. For a time Madrona grew with new Black members, but the anger and hurt was so deep that new people were not willing to stay for long. The fact that First Presbyterian Church had refused to allow Martin Luther King to speak in their building during this same period meant that African Americans did not see the Presbyterian Church as a place for them.

After a couple of years, the Grace people found themselves alone in the Madrona building, a building they did not want and that needed major repairs. They were without their pastor and many of their friends were in other churches. They were very angry. The Presbytery did not respond to them, probably wanting to avoid the anger.

Any conversation was now filled with conflict. A "merger" had taken place, but no one knew what that meant or how it was to work. There were two very distinct stories and experiences, one version by White people and the other by Black people. There was no way to sort out the two stories because both thought something had happened that never occurred. The relationship with the Presbytery was broken and no one knew how to fix it. Various commissions were appointed to solve the Madrona problem. This Gordian knot remained intractable. Sometimes these commissions expressed the threat or represented the threat of closing Madrona. That was what Daisy had meant.

They told us the stories with great reluctance. Several of them said that they had tried before and had always been rejected and even ridiculed. They had felt retribution when they had made earlier attempts. They learned to keep quiet and to go along; they feared the consequences of doing otherwise.

These are people with great integrity, faithfulness and conviction. They have served the Presbyterian Church all of their lives in spite of experiences that were hurtful and painful. They provided leadership to the Presbytery and remained loyal to it, even though that same Presbytery had treated them very badly.

After about three hours on that second Saturday morning Ivan and I thanked them and left feeling great pain and hurt. I asked them if they would be willing to continue telling their stories; we needed to hear them. Daisy, Gladys, the Rosses and some others agreed to continue meeting. This went on in my office for about a year. I began to urge them to tell the story to the Presbytery. This they were not willing to do. They had tried before and weren't going there again. After a couple of months they agreed to tell the story on video provided they had control of its content and use. The only way they would consider doing the video was that they would speak in generalities and would not name individuals involved. The video was theirs and in their control. They insisted that it could be used only with their permission and consent. We agreed.

We secured a video production company and the video was completed. The first time I saw the video I realized it was very restrained and left our most of the stories they had told me in the past year. I must confess I was a bit disappointed, but it was their story and their video.

I had also asked them if they would be willing to lead a service of Apology and Reconciliation. It became very clear that until they told their story, this would be a crippled and damaged church. Until they were able to provide the platform for reconciliation they would never be able to be an effective or strong congregation. The consequences of racism divided them among themselves and left a residual anger that drove strangers away. The African American community ridiculed their willingness to remain Presbyterian, a church that obviously wanted nothing to do with African Americans.

A service of apology and repentance would be a first step toward healing. This was something that the Presbytery could request but could not lead. Only those who have been the victim of racism can decide whether to invite the perpetrator to apologize, repent and reconcile. Victims propose reconciliation and forgiveness, not those who have committed the acts that created the victims. The Truth and Reconciliation process in South Africa arose from the Black South Africans, not the White South Africans.

The elders of Madrona agreed to discuss this idea and tentatively decided to do it on Pentecost, 2003. In the meantime, their full search for a new pastor had found an exciting candidate. The Pastor Nominating Committee proposed her name to the Committee on Ministry and we realized that a very able and gifted African American woman who was also a seminary professor was a wonderful gift to Madrona and the Presbytery. This process delayed the service of Apology, Repentance and Reconciliation.

Mercer Island Presbyterian Church responded with great care and concern and immediately acknowledged that they had been the beneficiary of this sad story, at the expense of Madrona. Remarkably, Mercer Island had formed a partnership with Madrona before we knew this story. They became full partners in this process and even though Mercer Island people had not been part of the decision making process regarding the money from Grace, they recognized their complicity. Mercer Island Presbyterian Church stood with the Presbytery in the apology and repentance.

The process began in which the minutes of all of the commissions were read and the search for documents that might help us understand the Presbytery actions and circumstances involved in this painful story.

I met with the priest of St. Clements Episcopal Church. A similar merger had taken place between Advent Episcopal Church which was African American and St. Clements which was White. The stories contained common themes and experiences. Both events took place at approximately the same time. A service of reconciliation between the Episcopal Diocese and St. Clements was held in the late 1990s. The experience of these two congregations was very helpful to us in our planning. We learned that reconciliation was a matter for the congregation to consider and initiate the necessary steps with the Presbytery. Of course, they might decide not to initiate such a process. This was their choice, not ours. We learned that the victims control the situation, not the perpetrators.

Flora Wilson Bridges, the new pastor, and the session began planning the service. They asked that I write a statement of apology and repentance. Dale Sewall, Pastor of Mercer Island Presbyterian Church, was asked to make a statement as well. We knew nothing more of the service than that. It was as it should be. This was their service and we were the apologetic and repentant guests. What if they do not accept our apology? What if they thank us for participating and cannot forgive us. It was not a pleasant thought, but who could blame them? This story was 50 years long. In fact, I began to wonder why they would forgive us. All any of us knew was that this had to be the first step and we did not know what the second step might be.

The service was held on World Communion Sunday, 2003. There were African American traditions employed, the Kenyan Choir sang, and joyful worship took place. It was a powerful two hours. The Madrona membership received us, they heard our apology and our repentance and they embraced us. We talked about how we would work at being faithful to our repentance and that we would need their help. To my amazement they responded that they would need to work and change to fulfill the reconciliation as well. We left Madrona that night with a feeling of hope and challenge that we will never forget.

We would soon learn that the first step and the easiest step in the reconciliation process had been taken. We were about to learn how many more and far more difficult steps would be required.

Good intentions, bad outcomes

Racism in the United States is always hidden and under cover. The early events of this story took place in the very early 1950s, when racism was blatant. Eugenics had only recently fallen out of favor. Schools were not yet desegregated, fair housing was not possible, and equal employment opportunity would not become law for another decade. There may have been good intentions on the part of the Presbytery, but in this context those good intentions meant little. Racism was blatantly present in the Madrona congregation, and the broken promises reflected the lack of respect for African Americans in general.

Remarkably the people of Grace had lived in White culture in their education and in their church. They were a small minority in a predominantly White denomination. Seattle Presbytery reflected that same pattern. Even though they saw themselves as loyal to the Presbyterian Church they were treated as outsiders. When they used the Book of Order to defend themselves they were resented and were accused of using it for their own ends.

For many years good people were trying to be helpful to Madrona. They did not intend to be racist and didn't know they were. The greatest example of this phenomenon was that commission after commission told them what to do and refused to listen to or believe the pain and anger being expressed. Minutes of these commissions are replete with ideas, plans and programs to facilitate growth. Training of leaders was a constant theme; strong elders would bring this church to life. The blanket conclusion that no one would ever treat fellow Presbyterians in a racist way formed the denial that prevented hearing the anger of the Madrona people. The minutes do not record any conversation regarding the anger of the Madrona people, nor the reasons for the anger. There is no evidence that the Madrona people were ever heard. Part of the story of Madrona is the pain of having attempted to tell their story and explain their anger only to be ignored, put down and accused of playing the victim role.

Ivan and I heard the story for the first time and consequently did not bring any experience, conclusion or defense regarding that story. The notion that a merger had taken place was not an idea we held. Reading of the minutes was easy for us; the lens of the supposed merger did not get in the way.

The value of these stories is to hear them and learn how racism works in this unintentional way. This is the gift that Madrona provides to us now. We have the opportunity to learn our own and current racism for we are no doubt doing what our predecessors did as they tried to be faithful.

We had to understand that White Americans do not live in nor do they share the culture of African Americans. We assume they do, and that they will be okay when they get it right. We want to tell them what to do and they want us to listen and know who they are. There is a huge gulf between us that they recognize and we do not. They have learned not to confront us. Confrontation only makes things more difficult for them. They try to appease us and we keep trying to get them to conform. Until we understand this, we lack integrity in our relationships with them and in much that we do with them.

We as the church are called to be agents of reconciliation. This experience has taught me how painful that is. We too easily accept being agents of reconciliation. We reduce it to getting people to like each other, to shake hands and move on. It is, however, much more than that. It requires recognition of wrongs committed. It requires listening to those hurt by those wrongs, hearing their pain and anger, pain and anger caused by us. This is difficult, yet reconciliation is not possible any other way.

The Matter of Reparations

We did not use the word "reparations." No one in Madrona ever asked us for anything. They did not insist that we meet the past promises of building repairs and the matter never arose. We felt compelled following the service of apology to respond in a way other than saying we were sorry. We had been working for about a year to replace the roof on the building. We encouraged them to get bids for the roof project so we could proceed. Prior to the service of Apology this issue just dragged on without resolution. They had heard this promise before and I doubt they trusted it this time.

The next week after the Service of Apology, Jack Van Hartesvelt, an elder in the Mercer Island Presbyterian Church, called me. He was so moved by the story of Madrona he wanted to do the same thing for Madrona. He calculated that the Mercer Island building was worth about a million dollars and had been made possible at the expense of Madrona. He wanted to put a million dollars worth of remodeling into the Madrona building. This essentially involved gutting much of the building and remodeling it. Most of that work was completed on two weekends in March, 2004. Volunteer craftsmen, new equipment and building materials donated by suppliers and volunteers from the Presbytery turned the old rather dilapidated building into a very attractive and appealing church.

Reparations were required and it was more than just a new roof. The Madrona members had worshipped in this building that needed major work for 50 years and it had not happened. It was important that we keep the promise that had been made.

This event closed the past for Madrona, Mercer Island and the Presbytery. The past experience could now be left in the past. We could now stand in a new doorway leading to the future. It would be easy to believe the work of reconciliation had been completed, but it had in fact only now begun. Reconciliation is not possible until the past is told, repented of and accounted for. All that had happened had only made reconciliation possible; now the hard work would begin, this we knew. Remarkably all that had taken place had fallen into place as we lived it together. There was no master plan, or step by step process that had gotten us to this point. We knew we would live in this together for a long time, but we did not know what would happen or how it would happen. We just knew that we had connected in a way that we could not let slip away.

The Consequences of Racism

When a group, organization or individuals experience racist comments, behaviors or actions, complex consequences are the result.

Repressed Anger

Racism produces anger and intimidates angry responses. The anger becomes embedded in organizations and individuals. Expression of this anger is very dangerous and risky. Retribution has been and often still is very severe. A person who would actually express this anger must be put in his or her place. Lynching was common well into the Twentieth Century.

Mental health professionals have affirmed the destructive power of repressed anger. Physical and mental health, social and interpersonal relationship, organizational and community networks are all weakened and put at risk. I believe we have paid less attention and often don't even acknowledge the impact on organizations.

Organizational Consequences

Dissension and Division

Anger may be repressed but that anger will be expressed in some way and at sometime. Repressed anger will be detached from the causal event and as a result be difficult to resolve. Unrelated incidents will trigger expressions of the anger. The safe settings will be used for these angry outbursts. Churches, community groups and civil rights organization are safe. The work place, general public meetings and court rooms are not. The safe settings cannot or will not exact retribution. This human dynamic has been used very effectively against those oppressed by racism. This was the primary strategy used by the slave owners, as we have seen in Chapter Five. The apartheid government of South Africa used the same strategy.

Creating dissension within the oppressed group produces the primary object of racial domination. If the victim community remains fractured and divided it is easily controlled. No threat will emerge from a united effort as long as people do not trust one another.

This means organizations are filled with dissension and division which threatens the effectiveness and strength of that organization. Often when an organization begins to find new strength and effectiveness, the dissension and division will increase. The dissension and division is a result of repressed anger, and may have little to do with the actual content of the issue being addressed. At the very least, anger regarding any issue will be elevated more than the issue warrants.

Decision Making Processes

Decision making is filled with irony. If a process for decision making has been adopted, some will attempt to work within it and others will not. The old division problem will persist. When a process is named and outlined, the focus is likely to shift to mistakes made in the process rather than in the outcome of the decision. This is a trait of the human family. However, it is a more common trait in communities that have been victims of racism.

The irony is that the very means to arrive at fair and balanced decision making becomes the problem. When that decision making process breaks down, appeals will frequently be made to outside authorities to resolve the matter. Most often these outside authorities represent the larger White institution. This response provides the opportunity for the perpetrators of racism to exert the very control the victims fear the most. In these events the repressed anger increases and reasserts the division in the organization.

Difficulty for Leaders

We observed the issues of leadership as a result of the slave culture earlier. All we need recognize at this point is that leaders will frequently be caught in the midst of the dissension and division, and they will frequently be the target of the repressed anger.

Mistrust of Institutional Authority

This is certainly no surprise. Institutional authority is the very center of the racial domination. Reconciliation within institutions is very difficult as a result.

Role of Dominant Culture People

Dominant culture people may become part of an organization that has been a victim of racism. This can be a positive step in the reconciliation process. However, it can also become very destructive. The dominant culture people must learn multicultural skills and be very clear about their own motives and desires. They must not attempt to fix the organization and must not become the expert in solving problems. They must not provide leadership to any faction in the organization. They must be people who can affirm, encourage and support leadership. Full participation requires a consistent behavior that produces unity and understanding. When a dominant culture person becomes enmeshed in the dissension his or her best choice is to leave the organization.

The Consequences of Racism in Madrona

Madrona was dying. It was badly fractured and suspicious. The initial experience had taken place 50 years earlier, but was only a small part of the current reality. Attempts had been made by Madrona to express their hurt and anger and those attempts had been rejected or denied. The hurt was refueled each time they were not heard. They wanted to be heard. They wanted the Presbytery to know how they felt and why. Even when the Presbytery tried to help, the help was never at the core. Commissions made good suggestions, and adopted good strategies, but nothing ever changed. It didn't change because the core issue was never heard nor accepted. They were accused of lying and manipulating the truth. They were accused of playing the victim role, the race card. Each time the anger grew in them.

It also pitted them against each other. It is amazing to see the impact of racism, over and over again. It always results in pitting people against each other as they are treated in racist ways. The film, *Hotel Rwanda,* is another illustration. The Belgian colonizers made a distinction based on lightness of skin and width of nose to create a privileged class called the Tutsi. The Hutu were the excluded. Prior to the arrival of the Belgians this was not a matter of significance. In the early 1990's this resulted in an attempted genocide by the Hutu's against the Tutsi. This is always one of the consequences of racism. We see it in South Africa, the United States and in Western Europe. It is also true in Asia and Southeast Asia. This same reality made it impossible for Madrona to ever have an effective life as a congregation or to provide ministry to a larger community. This had to be healed in Madrona before anything could grow and flourish.

The confirmation of this can be seen in the life of Madrona in the year following the Service of Apology and Reconciliation. The membership grew significantly in a congregation at ease and in healthy relationships with each other. The story they told has little importance to them now. They have often said,"It's over, we have been heard, and we now have the responsibility to live into reconciliation". The transformation is quite remarkable, and none of that transformation has come from the Presbytery, except an apology and a desire to find reconciliation.

Racism is a virus in our community and organizational life. That virus continues to separate, deceive and violate people. We are all crippled and immobilized by it. We will not be what we could be as long as that virus is active among us. We will remain weakened, hoping for a hero, until we decide to end it. It is a choice we can make. We can end it.

CHAPTER SEVEN

The Difficulty of Reconciliation

It's not handshakes and smiles all around.

Reconciliation is a concept that is very appealing. Resolution of conflict, healing of relationships and injustice, overcoming hatred and abuse are all goals of the quest of the Arthur myth. Setting people free from evil is a persistent theme. For those who endure the hurt, the hatred and the abuse, peace and reconciliation is a dream that seems more like fantasy with each new hurt. Why is it that reconciliation is so difficult? Doesn't everyone desire it?

Even though it is desirable, the task becomes immensely complex when attempted. This complexity derives from the two groups seeking reconciliation, the offender and the offended. The offending group must first recognize the wrong they have committed, repent of that behavior, apologize for that behavior and ask forgiveness. This is a huge hurdle for a culture that perceives itself as just and compassionate, destined to set all things right. The recognition of having committed such acts requires an awareness of history and one's self that is discouraged by loud and strong voices in that society and culture. Further it is unlikely that all members of the offending group will agree about the offense, its nature or its details. When well intentioned people try to provide the right and proper solutions, it is difficult to understand the resistive response or the recurring anger. These same well-intentioned people need explanations and reasons for this response. Most of the time, the answers they find serve to confirm their own racism and deepen resentment of African Americans. A common example of this problem is the conviction that African Americans play the race card and act as victims when they want something. This allows the offending group to dismiss African American claims and anger as well as the reality of racism. In takes little time before the conversation turns to defensive denial and paternalism. The ensuing arguments about what took place and why, consumes much of the energy required to start the journey toward reconciliation. Reconciliation is lost before the first step is taken.

This denial and failure to understand stifles the voices that are most able to articulate the reasons for resistive responses, those who were hurt and offended. Those who can best recognize and illustrate the behaviors of racism are those who are the victims of it. Yet these are the same victims whose integrity and honesty are defamed and denied. It is they who have been discounted as unworthy and unreliable. Can those who have been victims of the behavior, the least powerful, tell the powerful of the offense committed against them? It has and is happening in South Africa, but can it happen in the United States? Perhaps, in certain places and at certain times it can. More problematical it suggests that the victims carry the burden to heal those who have victimized them. When this happens the courage and conviction of the offended are immense.

But why is this their burden and responsibility? The ultimate act of arrogance is to suggest they must solve our problem and we will wait for their action to do so. If they can tell us the truth while not offending us or hurting our feelings maybe we will listen to them. They do carry a burden that we placed on them. We must remove that burden and address our own racism if we intend to take the tiniest first steps toward reconciliation.

The offended group has learned how to survive in the face of these behaviors and live with consequences that are divisive for them. They are scarred and wounded and do not easily trust. They may not trust each other, and they certainly do not trust the offenders. Yet some level of trust is essential for the offended group to even risk telling their experiences to the powerful group that has committed the offense. It is unlikely that everyone in the offended group experienced the events the same way. The consequence of the behavior toward them has resulted in fracturing, defensiveness, and survival strategies. The offended group must take steps to be vulnerable, which seems insane. They are already quite vulnerable and have been for a long time.

If we assume people from both of these groups actually do seek reconciliation, the hard work has only begun. The healing process requires engagement - - serious engagement. Hearing and receiving what has been denied is painful. Offering the story of the pain to those who may be skeptical or practicing pain avoidance is frustrating and rips the scabs off old wounds. To sit together with the proposition that this will be the nature of our time together produces anxiety, fear and clumsiness. One group hoping to preserve denial is confronted by those who are survivors of the experience and articulate its violence and brutality. Two groups who have lived in inequality must now live in equality. None of the patterns or assumptions that inform our social, political or economic life together offer insights about how to do this. Old patterns will continue until each one is systematically undone. This is a commitment of immense energy, candor, trust and time.

As this process works new offenses may take place, the process is always in jeopardy. This is made all the more difficult when the offending group does not even recognize the wrongness of the behaviors and does not intend to offend. Lack of self awareness in the offending group when coupled with the reticence of the offended to speak leaves the same dark chasm between us, even as we sit together attempting to build a bridge across it.

While the dynamic exists, we must find ways through it, there is much at stake. If the reconciliation fails, the mistrust will grow, the behaviors will become ever more entrenched in both the survival culture and conquest culture. The gap will continue to widen and make future attempts at reconciliation more complex and difficult.

It was at this precise point that despair began to grow within me. Perhaps it is not achievable. Are we doomed to live in the consequences of the past, transporting racism into the future? Is it actually a circle that we race around, but never change? If we understand two cultures and the clash between them, and if we understand the history and acknowledge its brutality, can we not end the consequences?

The Confrontation

How would it be possible for the Presbytery of Seattle to hear the stories of the people of Madrona? They had tried to tell the story before and had been rejected; they certainly were not willing to stand before several hundred people and try again. They did agree to tell the story through video. A production company, White Noise Productions was secured and a very fine video was produced and interestingly titled *We Were Born Presbyterian*. The first public showing of the video was at the November 2003 Seattle Presbytery meeting. The people of Madrona were especially invited to be in attendance. Before the video was shown I told the

Presbytery that we would not engage in a discussion of the video that night with 200 people involved. This was the time for the Presbytery to listen and reflect. We would have opportunity later to discuss it in various forums. The room was silent at the conclusion of the video; the Presbytery had listened and they heard.

In early January we left on a second trip to South Africa. With the Christmas season following the Presbytery meeting there had been individual affirmation of the video and churches were planning how to use it in January and in the coming months. Little other response was made. Forums for discussing the video were scheduled for late January and throughout the spring.

Upon returning from South Africa I was told that the minutes of the Presbytery had been carefully researched by the Presbytery Historian and a couple of other individuals. Their conclusion was that the story told by the people of Madrona was not true. The minutes did not reflect anything that was said on the video. I received a long and detailed account of that research and was grateful for it.

This difficult and tedious work illustrated the first and primary difficulty in reconciliation. White people assume that the truth about an event is included in the written record such as minutes of meetings. The promises made were not mentioned, the failure to keep the promises was not mentioned and the ways in which Mercer Island benefited were oblique at best. Having listened to the Madrona people for more than a year, I could rather easily fill in the blanks. I realized the response that I was receiving was the response that Madrona had always received when they attempted to describe their experiences.

The response to the confrontation by some was denial that any part of the story was true, and implied that the renovation of Madrona was based on fraudulent intent.

Somehow, the Black folks got it wrong again, either deliberately to get something they wanted, or their memory was faulty. A specific group of people who represented the White perspective, (I didn't know who or how many), were very unsettled and angry over the whole issue. They accused me of having betrayed them. For the next six months, I would hear of them, but still did not know who they were. They refused to have any contact with me or to discuss the video. It was my conviction that if we could talk, I would be able to tell what I had heard at Madrona and what it meant. Certainly they would understand and want to be part of the reconciliation process. It seemed obvious that whoever they were they had had direct involvement with Madrona in the past. Whatever that involvement had been, unintentional racism had taken place.

In the video the Madrona people did not use names because they did not want to vilify individuals; they wanted only to share their anger, pain and hurt. They did not want to get into a good White people vs. bad White people debate. While they had been treated very badly by some, the important point was that no one would listen to them

This behavior is very typical when the issue of race surfaces. Denial and offense are the first reactions; denial that any of it is true and being offended that anyone would suggest that they did anything that was racist.

Denial and offense is followed by avoidance and refusal to communicate. This was very frustrating for me; I can only imagine the frustration of African Americans who have tolerated this for centuries.

About six months after the showing of the video, I began insisting that this group of people, whoever they were, meet with me. I did receive an invitation to meet with them and was told that I could only listen and not speak. While this did not bode well for a conversation, I agreed since at least we could finally begin a conversation. In the course of that meeting some of the things I was told were:

- Not to call them good well intentioned people; "that was just pap trying to appease them."

- "You were conned by the people of Madrona; they only want to use the Book of Order when it suits their purposes."

- "They are not to be trusted, they have manipulated you."

- "The story about money going to Mercer Island is the way they play the race card."

- "I will never speak to them until they apologize to me for the way I was treated."

- "The video must be withdrawn from use; you must apologize for allowing it to be made."

After about two hours, I told them I would need to leave in about fifteen minutes. They had completed their presentations at that point and allowed me to speak. I told them that I was glad to have finally been able to meet with them, that I had wanted to do so for a long time. The response was, "After all we have just said to you, why are you attacking us suggesting we wouldn't meet with you?"

As I left that meeting I realized I had experienced in a very small way exactly what the people of Madrona had experienced for 50 years. Dialogue about these issues would not be allowed. Responses to any comment I made would be deflected to another issue, or there would be long speeches explaining why I am wrong. My experience was different than the people of Madrona, because I could leave and go on with my day, and African Americans leave one experience to enter another, and another.

The racism was classic in the events that surrounded Madrona... The Presbytery had attempted to strengthen Madrona as a church while denying the past and assuming that African Americans are unable to perform at an appropriate level. Of course, this is the classic confrontation between conquest culture people and survival culture people. If African American will act like us, and become life us then they will succeed. However, since they are not like us they are not trustworthy and hope to get what they want by playing the victim role. The people of Madrona learned to say what the White people wanted to hear, while doing what they wanted to do. White culture in the guise of Presbyterianism was informing African Americans how to be a church even though they were raised and nurtured in the Presbyterian Church. So strong were they in their Presbyterianism that they stayed loyal to it even in the midst of racist actions toward them. The Presbytery intentions were good; the behaviors were not recognized as racist. Black folks have told us and told us that we just don't get it. They are right.

Bishop Desmond Tutu reflects on this question in his book, *No Future Without Forgiveness,* "How was it possible for normal, decent, and God-fearing people, as White South Africans considered themselves to be, to have turned a blind eye to a system which impoverished, oppressed, and violated so many of those others with whom they shared the beautiful land that was their common motherland?"[29] This could just as well say how was it possible for normal, decent, and God-fearing people, as White Americans considered themselves to be, have turned a blind eye to a system which impoverished, oppressed and violated so many others in Seattle Presbytery?

This is the first difficulty in reconciliation. When we are confronted we want to deny. Feelings get hurt, and we don't like that. Of course, suggesting to African Americans that we don't want to listen and have our feelings hurt is not likely to bring much sympathy. We have hurt their feelings and a lot worse for centuries. We can probably survive the experience; it was a serious question as to whether they would. The more we have worked at overcoming racism the harder it is for us to face the racism in ourselves. The process of reconciliation will not ever be able to hold an event, discussion or process that result in everyone being reconciled. We will all come to that moment at different times and in different ways. There will always be denial and avoidance on the part of White people. Reconciliation in South Africa continues even though it was addressed by a whole nation following the horror of Apartheid. It will be even more difficult in the United States because slavery ended a long time ago.

An important first learning is that reconciliation processes are impossible to fulfill in the face of denial of the very events that are at the source of the issues. Part of this problem arises out of our cultural differences. White people are inclined to base decisions on recorded data and information. African Americans rely upon experience, memory and feelings.

Information is retained and repeated in very different ways. It is no wonder that African Americans and euro Americans can observe the same event and report two very different and distinct happenings Reports of that event may not even have the same focal point. Northern European culture does not trust or believe oral traditions and will reject the African American description as unreliable. Ironically, the reliance upon the written word is often less reliable than is the oral tradition. Minutes of meetings include the information that is chosen to be preserved.

Embarrassing information or statements counter to our own self image will be left out.

The Critical Moment

As was mentioned earlier, Jack Vanhartesvelt, an elder in Mercer Island Presbyterian Church, wanted to return the benefit that had been gained at the expense of Madrona. He proposed that he gather skilled crafts people, donated equipment and materials and renovate the Madrona building. This miracle worker recruited an architectural firm that worked pro bono and labor unions who donated skilled laborers. Businesses donated kitchen appliances, siding, paint, and all necessary materials. In two weekends the skilled laborers and a host of volunteers completely remodeled and renovated the Madrona building. One of the local restaurants even donated the meals for the workers on both weekends. A video of this work was also created, and every time I speak on that video I use the word "amazing." I still get teased about it. The word was accurate; I <u>was</u> amazed.

Madrona worshipped with Mercer Island during the renovation of the building. Many of us believed that when Dr. Flora Wilson Bridges, the pastor of Madrona, preached the sermon, it would be celebratory of what had been accomplished. The building was being renovated, reconciliation had happened and now it was time to be congratulated and appropriately thanked. But Dr. Bridges did not do this. She preached a sermon that stated the hurt and anger of African Americans. She spoke strongly of the need for reparations and the continuing consequences of racism in this country. Dr. Bridges is a very articulate and strong preacher. The message was heard.

Some people described this as extreme while others thought it was unfairly harsh. Many did understand and responded with appreciation, which frankly surprised me. There was tension in Mercer Island. We had reached a critical moment in the reconciliation process. White culture tends to sequence events; there is a beginning, middle and an end. Issues are encountered, identified and analyzed. The solution to the problem is outlined, planned, implemented and completed. We have solved the problem and the matter is now closed.

Reconciliation, however, has many beginnings and ends, and is continuous. It is uncertain whether any of us will live long enough to see it completed. In many respects the first steps of reconciliation bring us to an even more intense and challenging time. We are forced to shift from past events to the reality of present events. Now it is about us. Now we must confront the racism that is in all of us. Will we continue? Will we allow the persecuted to point at our racism and continue to challenge us? Will we allow them to speak of the continuing consequences of centuries of racism?

While it may have been disturbing and difficult to hear that sermon, the good news was that she trusted us and felt safe enough with us to tell us the truth, to tell us how she felt and saw the world. She was able to do this from the pulpit of Mercer Island Presbyterian Church. This was a huge step for all of us.

We need to recognize that the process of reconciliation provides a huge release of pressure for African Americans. This is pressure from a lifetime of stuffing down anger and hurt. They have learned well while in contact with us to keep us from recognizing that anger. They have never been allowed to tell us how they feel, the hurt they have because of us. All we have done so far is lifted the lid a little bit by giving a sense of safety for them to express the rage, anger and hurt they feel. It is probably something like shaking a coke and then opening the lid a little bit.

Our predictable response is to deny or avoid, as it has always been. We want to hide in a cave hoping it will go away. They are wrong, extreme, demanding and unfair, we say. We can't believe that is all true. Or we avoid the issue by affirming that they are right about everybody else's racism and we are willing to point out racism that is everyone's but our own. It is kind of fun to see racism in everything, even if it isn't there; it provides a wonderful diversion from confronting ourselves.

This is the critical moment where reconciliation will be most vulnerable to failure. I suspect this is why reconciliation efforts have begun, but often not finished. The questions for us are these. Will we engage the anger, hurt and rage? Will we listen and give them the opportunity to express fully that rage so that they can heal from the anger and we can learn of our own racism? If we can, then we have the possibility of engaging in an honest dialogue that will actually begin to end racism.

I must acknowledge that as hard and as painful as the Madrona process has been, we were in the best of possible situations. We had strong and effective pastors in Mercer Island, Dale Sewall, Sheri Edwards Dalton, and Paul Barrett. We had a strong and healthy congregation at Mercer Island and we had courageous leaders. We had a strong, effective and articulate pastor at Madrona in Flora Wilson Bridges. We were confronted by courageous, committed and faithful people in Madrona. We were all Presbyterians, we all knew each other and had worked together. What more could we ask for? How could there be a more ideal opportunity to confront racism? On several occasions I said to people that as hard as this is, we are not attempting to reconcile with angry Black young men in a ghetto.

We must acknowledge the greater difficulty in situations that do not have all of these gifts. People who have experienced racism can tell us when we have done "it" again, and we can learn to quit doing "it." The pain does not go away. Reconciliation has been for us an experience that has built hope and given new life. However, it has also deepened the sense of how hard reconciliation will be to achieve throughout our society. Yet, a taste of reconciliation drives us to desire more of it.

The reconciliation process forces us recognize that truth will never be validated by ignorance or denial. "Sometimes truth is easily recognizable and other times you have to dig deep to uncover it. You'll never find truth if you are afraid of the dark, afraid to search the thoughts in the inner recesses of your mind and get your hands dirty. When you find the truth, it may not be easy to recognize it because it's all covered with crud. You may have to chip the crud away, and wash and polish your new-found truth before you can recognize its intrinsic beauty and value."[30] Reconciliation will require getting our hands dirty while we do a lot of crud chipping.

The Collapse of Communication

Even in the ideal situation in which we were working, there were still many times conversations concluded with increased mistrust, frustration and anger. We must understand this tendency toward communication collapse. It will be even more present in less ideal situations. The desire to continue reconciliation processes drives us to recognize that consequences of racism act as the great protector of racism. As we have seen, the history of these two cultures is filled with exploitation, suspicion, hatred, violence, guilt, anger, and brutality. We have begun to realize that the two cultures use very different lenses to see the world. We have been able to move into a reconciliation process. We have recognized that reconciliation has many places in which we can stumble. What is it that so frequently derails our communication? It is the belief that we know what each other is thinking before any words are spoken.

The great protector of racism is the result of our history as two cultures. We think we know what the other's perception is and we hold it as rigid truth. We conclude that we know what they are thinking and what they think of us, and therefore we know why they do what they do. These perceptions are laid down layer upon layer upon layer. So, is it true that the sins of our fathers are visited upon their children to the third and fourth generation as is stated in Exodus? If so, then it is hopeless. We will need a non-racist generation to off set such a fate for three or four generations. Or is Paul correct in Romans in the affirmation of grace given by God, grace given to each other? It seems that Exodus is right so far, but what will bring Romans into play and offer us hope? The critical moment presents a choice: healthy communication or the collapse of communication.

Corey Schlosser Hall, the Communication Director for Seattle Presbytery, gave me a video and asked me to review it regarding communication issues. The video was entitled *Easy for You to Say*. The speaker was Randy Harrington, PhD, the CEO of Extreme Arts and Sciences. Toward the end of that video I had an "ah ha" moment. Randy described the ideas of R.D. Laing in his book, *Interpersonal Relations*. Laing pointed to both the problem and its solution. It struck me as odd that I had not sought the solution to my questions from communication resources earlier. This is a communication issue in a most profound way.

As we have said earlier, cultures tend to be exclusive. Each is rich with traditions and values; each has insights that can widen the human experience. The differences can enrich us all. "Here is the glory and wonder and mystery, yet too often we simply wish to ignore or destroy those points of view that refract light differently from our own."[31] Two cultures clash as each tries to ignore or destroy the differences, and failing that, denial of their veracity.

Persistent criticism and negative responses will build a barrier of mistrust and the reverse is also true. If we encounter affirmation from another person, we are likely to respond in positive ways and trust will grow. "We may not know ourselves as we are known, but we are constantly acting in the light of the actual or supposed attitudes, opinions, needs, and so on the other has in respect to (us)."[32] My experiences of the responses of others to me alter my self identity and my perception of how others view me. We have all experienced the difference in relationships between the affirming supportive person and the negative critical person. Close trusting relationships are not built with persons who continually criticize, attack and bully us.

These exchanges create two identities: Self-identity (my view of myself) and meta-identity (my view of your view of me) which is informed by our cultural mores and biases. "Self identity is constituted not only by our looking at ourselves, but also by our looking at others looking at us and our reconstitution and alteration of these views of the others about us. At this more complex, more concrete level, self identity is a synthesis of my looking at me with my view of other's view of me."[33] Desmond Tutu makes the same point. "We are bound up in a delicate network of interdependence because, as we say in our African idiom, a person is a person through other persons."[34] Stereotypes inform the perception of the motives of other groups of people. Stereotypes build a network of biases that define the behaviors of all individuals in that group. The bias is received by those in the other group and becomes part of their self identity.

Perception of motive determines behavior. Laing proposes there are actually six people present when two people meet: You and me, my perception of you and your perception of me, my perception of your perception of me, and your perception of my perception of you. We think we know what the other is thinking of us and therefore we know their motive. In response to this perceived motive we behave in ways to protect ourselves or deny their perceptions. This will lead to their stronger assertion of their position insisting that they are not doing what we perceive they are doing. Their denial of our perception of them will be a stronger defense on our part and a persistent denial of their perceptions. Laing calls this the "spiral of reciprocating perceptions." People act toward each other based on their perception of what they think the other person is thinking about them.

We can apply this to conversations between White and Black people, and in fact probably have been in this spiral ourselves at various times. "One or both persons in a twosome may spiral off into third, fourth, even fifth levels of what we have suggested may be called meta-perceptions. Such a spiral develops for instance, whenever two persons mistrust each other."[35] Laing recognizes that what is true for individuals is true for groups as well.

Here is an artificial illustration. I have made it up, but I suspect it has actually taken place thousands of times. An African American man is seated by the window of the bus; the aisle seat is empty. At the next stop a Northern European man boards the bus and the only empty seat is next to the African American. The African American is reading the local African American newspaper and has put part of it on the empty seat. Let's do a quick reality check before we go on with the story. The African American would not necessarily be aware that there is only one empty seat on the bus. The empty seat was a convenient place to put the part of the paper he had already read. The Northern European wanted to sit down for any number of possible reasons. He may be tired, has a bad back or a sore foot.

What perceptions do these two men have of each other? Does the Black man wonder why the White man has decided he has to sit in that seat? The Black man assumes the White man will just sit down; paper or no paper. He hurriedly grabs his paper from the seat. The White man thinks the Black man doesn't want him to sit down because he wants to use that seat for his own minor convenience. He is obviously upset; he jerked his paper from the seat and didn't say anything to him...

The White man takes the seat; they do not speak. As the bus ride continues the Black man's perception is that the White man perceives him as second class and not even worthy of a polite request or greeting. The White man's perception is that the Black man thinks he is a racist and doesn't want to say anything to him.

When the bus arrives at the Black man's destination he struggles to get his large briefcase from behind his legs. Finally he is able to stand. He hurries to the aisle, fearing the driver will not know he wants to get off. The White man slowly turns in the seat but does not stand up. This makes the task of getting the briefcase and himself out much more difficult for the Black man; however he must get to the aisle quickly. As he struggles he bumps the White man with the briefcase and nearly trips. The White man does not offer any help and scowls when hit by the briefcase. As the Black man reaches the aisle he mutters something that sounds to the White man like "arrogant blankety blank." The White man thinks he knows the word that followed "arrogant". He responds, "I would have moved if you had asked and not been so rude." The Black man shrugs and gets to the door as the driver starts to close it but does manage to get off. Both men have had their perceptions confirmed and both feel alienated. Any further conversation at that moment would result in the spiral of reciprocal perception erupting in anger, frustration and perhaps even violence.

Play with this scenario: Would this change:

- If the White man was sitting by the window?
- If the Black man was 20 years old and the White man was elderly?
- If the Black person sitting on the aisle is an elderly woman and the seat next to the window is empty?
- If the Black person is well dressed?
- If the Black person is dressed in very dirty work clothes?
- If the White man is a laborer and the Black man is dressed as a successful businessman?

There are many possible scenarios. I suspect the only difference in the outcomes will be a matter of intensity. After all, does it matter that the car in the exclusive White neighborhood is filled with teenage Black girls, a Black businessman that lives in the neighborhood, or an elderly Black couple? It is likely they will be stopped and questioned by the police regardless of these factors.

The Academy Award winning movie *Crash* is a powerful and graphic portrayal of the spiral of reciprocal perceptions. Each link in this chain of events begins with the spiral and the consequences are consistent. My only complaint about the movie is that it has a happy ending. Most of the time the ending is tragic. As I watched this movie I knew the more common tragic outcome. Nonetheless, it is a great movie that R. D. Laing would be using in his classrooms.

Conquest and survival cultures establish the basis for misunderstanding and mistrust before we even meet or begin to converse. The biases and stereotypes are in play when we see each other. Previous experiences, history, and cultures interact and form our attitudes that are on display when we encounter each other. The dynamic is at work although we haven't uttered a word. We don't perceive reality the same way. It is as though we have come from two different planets. We experience a common event, but do not see that event the same way at all. Our cultures are in conflict and usually we can turn to cross cultural skills to help us. My experience in cross cultural settings is that most immigrant communities know how to do this very well. They have already learned these skills as they entered and survived in our culture. It is usually the White people who struggle to learn these skills and practice them.

Cross cultural skills and practices have been of little benefit as Blacks and White have attempted engagement. If we examine some of the cross cultural skills and practices we can see why this is so.

Some basic cross cultural skills and practices are:

1. Assume that the other person is acting on the basis of what they believe is right and is respectful of you.

   In our spiral of reciprocating perceptions we assume anything but this to be true.

2. Assume that you will need to change your behavior in order to create the space in which to meet each other. The other person will do so as well.

   Our behavior has already been changed by our perception of their perception of us.

3. In the church assume that this person is also a Christian who serves the same Lord; we are one body.

Sunday remains the most segregated place in our society.

4. Assume that your behavior and clothes are as funny and strange to them as theirs are to you.

This may be true, but tolerance, acceptance and appreciation are not the usual responses.

5. If they are speaking in a language other than your own, don't assume they are talking about you and are laughing at you. They are probably laughing at themselves or because they feel awkward.

No, they are not laughing at themselves. Neither party, White nor Black, sees any humor in any of it.

6. Understand that some of your behaviors are probably very offensive to them, and they are trying to understand your behavior.

Behavior is a response to the way we think we are perceived, and both think that they are perceived badly by the other. It may be that our behaviors are designed to offend each other.

7. Do not assume that they need your help; they may only need your friendship

In the midst of reconciliation processes this sounds absolutely silly.

Applying these skills to racial healing seems out of the question. The spiral of reciprocal perceptions continues to direct and determine our exchanges.

In some conversations regarding Madrona I found myself being drawn into a triangle that insisted I had to straighten out the thinking of the Madrona people, or I was being duped by their manipulation and disingenuous stories. "We know what they are thinking, we know their perception of our perception of them, and they are wrong." Any counter information, perspective or perception that I offered was quickly and abruptly dismissed. The spiral was at work before I even met the disgruntled group the first time. There was a wall and it was impenetrable. It was distressing, frustrating and discouraging. On the one hand reconciliation had and was taking place but on the other hand it was dismissed as fraudulent and meaningless.

Some of the statements made in these meetings illustrate the spiral of reciprocal perceptions. I indicated that the Madrona people making the video were determined to not use specific names as they did not want to demean individuals. The response was, "They don't want to be held accountable. That is why they didn't use any names. They never want to be accountable." When I recounted conversations with members of Madrona, the response was that the Madrona people were playing the victim card again. "They always want to be the victim. We don't believe in helping people who act like victims all of the time."

In the final analysis, whatever had happened for whatever reason, the only outcome was that the Madrona people had won and had gotten what they wanted. When I indicated that the Madrona people never asked for anything throughout these conversations, and that the building renovation was the idea of Jack Vanhartesvelt, they scoffed and accused me of lying.

It is important to recognize this same spiral in the people of Madrona. Daisy Dawson was certain that she knew what Ivan and I were thinking and the nature of our motives in that meeting. When she said to us, "The Presbytery has been trying to close this church for 50 years and we aren't going anywhere," the spiral was in place. The dialogue at the end of this chapter is an attempt to illustrate the development of the spiral of reciprocal perception between Madrona and the Presbytery.

The following exchange may seem familiar. An African American meets a European American and a conversation ensues. The European American believes the African American believes he/she is a racist. The African American believes the European American believes he/she is inferior. The European American is tentative as he/she greets the African American. The African American thinks the European American is tentative because he/she doesn't really want to engage; consequently the African American is uncomfortable and is tentative as well. The European American proceeds to ask a series of questions, such as "Where do you work, are you married, do you have children." The African American is not sure he/she wants to reveal all of this information and offers only cryptic answers. The European American presses for more information as a means to establish conversation. The African American is suspicious of the motive of the European American, "what is this person after? What do they want? This mistrust increases the reticence to respond... If either party makes any comment that can be interpreted as judgmental, the spiral becomes a tornado. For example, if the European American asks what the African American thinks about racial profiling, the African American may respond that it is a real problem. The Northern European may respond, "How else do we stop all this crime?" The White American will think the African American is taking a victim role and that the White American is the perpetrator of all that is bad in Black History. The African American will think that the White American doesn't get it and is the beneficiary of White privilege. The African American may even say, "You White people just don't get it." The possibility of a cordial and casual conversation ends in frustration and anger.

It is no wonder when we confront the big issues and glaring problems that we become utterly bogged down in miscommunication, mistrust, anger and frustration.

The longer the spiral of reciprocal perception infects the relationship between African Americans and European Americans; the deeper and wider is the chasm between them.

Our hope is in the fact that the spiral cannot continue if one group stops responding based on their perceptions of the other group. The power we all have is to refuse participation in the spiral. This was the decision of Black South Africans. The spiral is broken as soon as we decide to end it.

I remember well those encounters with Rudy Cuellar those many years ago in my first pastoral position in Roseville, CA. I remember and now realize how well he remained focused and magically avoided that spiral. He was honest, his anger was obvious, his intention was clear, but he never told me what he thought I was thinking. The avoidance of the spiral gave me the ability to confront my own racism. He chose not to enter that spiral of reciprocal perception just as the Black South Africans did 25 years later.

In an earlier time Ivan and I might very well have responded differently to the Madrona people. We might have seen the statements of Daisy and others as only whimpering by people who liked being victims. Had we shared some of this history or been part of some of the events we might have responded defensively and not heard what they were saying.

We didn't, because the Truth and Reconciliation Commission in South Africa had influenced us. Personal struggles with racism had already transpired in my life. Ivan and I interrupted the spiral of reciprocal perceptions by listening to the stories and respecting their integrity. The people of Madrona broke the spiral when they refused to make this a personal attack or a personal debate. In doing so, they provided the way for us to hear the stories and not engage the personal perceptions that would have prevented our listening. I didn't know we, or they had done this -- at the time, I had not yet heard of R. D. Laing.

Can we learn to listen before our perceptions and assumptions add to the alienation of broken relationships? That is the next step in our Quest.

The Dialogue

The following attempts to track the interaction between the Presbytery and Madrona. Read this and watch for the cycle of reciprocal perceptions at work.

Presbytery: Grace is a weak Black church and Madrona is a weak White church. If we were to merge them they both may be stronger. Besides, this would demonstrate our desire to integrate. (Remember this is 1953 and integration was the emerging issue of concern.)

Madrona: The people of Grace ask: Will we be accepted in Madrona?

Interaction

The Presbytery did not develop a merger plan or process. No merger agreement between the two sessions was ever adopted. The difficulties of integration were not anticipated nor was there a strategy to identify those issues, some of which were these issues were: division of power, decision making, participation in activities of the congregation, building maintenance needs.

The Grace congregation was worried about this proposal but would go along with it if the Presbytery determined that it would be the best option.

Presbytery: The people of Grace were assured that the funds from the sale of their building would be used to resolve serious maintenance issues at Madrona and that their pastor would become a staff member at Madrona. The meeting of the Presbytery did not take action to merge the two churches, but closed Grace, did not move the pastor of Grace to Madrona, and moved through a very convoluted process regarding the funds from Grace.

Madrona: Those funds did not go with the Grace members on Easter Sunday and they were treated rudely and rejected. Funds from the sale of Grace were used in part to do some small repair to Madrona, but the balance of the funds from the sale of Grace were combined with the funds transferred from Grace and the sale of real property and were used to buy the land for the Mercer Island Presbyterian Church.

Presbytery: The problem of Grace was solved and many members scattered to other churches. There was no black church in the presbytery; integration had been achieved.

Interaction

In the next meeting of the Presbytery, the Presbytery Executive stated that there had never been a plan for racial justice ministry and that no such strategy existed in the Presbytery. This statement was confusing as he had at the previous Presbytery meeting indicated this was the very reason the "merger" between Grace and Madrona was initiated.

The Madrona people begin to leave. This White flight left the congregation with a few White people and the Grace people.

Madrona: Angry and vulnerable, Grace people find themselves in a building they did not want, without a pastor and having lost many of their friends.

Interaction

White People: What more do they want? We have other work to do. Mercer Island will grow and generate income, Madrona will not. Its people are poor. We can't solve all of this. We need to teach them to function correctly so they can succeed.

Black People: The Presbytery only wants to control us. They lied to us because they think we are stupid and incapable. We have tried to make this work, and see what it got us.

Presbytery: The needs of the Madrona building are costly. There are many financial needs in the Presbytery. Congregations need to be responsible for their own buildings and Madrona is not different. We will loan them funds for a new roof but we will not give them funds to do this.

Madrona: The promised repairs are incomplete. Many problems need repair including the roof which is leaking badly. Funds have not been forthcoming for 10 years from the Presbytery. We feel betrayed. They lied to us. We are angry that our only option is a loan which we cannot afford.

Interaction

White People: What do they expect of us? They want a free ride. They are dependent and we must break this pattern. They need to get over "it", integration has occurred.

Black People: The Presbytery is a typical group of White people: you can't trust them. They don't listen to us, nothing has changed and we have been forced to be in a building we cannot afford to maintain.

Presbytery: Ten years after closing Grace, it denies that promises were made regarding the sale of the Grace building and denies that any funds went to Mercer Island. The stories told by people of Madrona are rejected, discredited and ridiculed.

Madrona: Conflict ensues. Due to their loyalty and tradition as Presbyterians, some want to keep trying to work with the Presbytery. Others want to keep their church and view the Presbytery as the enemy.

Interaction

White People: These people are not to be believed. They don't even know what they want. They are in conflict with each other and their pastor. This is a troubled church.

Black People: We are hurt and angry. We are Presbyterians, but we do not trust the system. What do we do? Do we pretend to get along with the Presbytery? Do we only act like we are doing what they want?

Presbytery: Commissions are appointed to get Madrona to function as they think it should. The Presbytery acts as if this is just another conflicted church. At times the session is even removed by the Presbytery. (Note: The conflict arises out of the hurt of the past. Usual conflict management processes will not work without listening to the stories of the past.)

Interaction

White People: We have met with them, we have helped them find pastors, and we have spent hours and hours with them. Nothing ever changes. We don't know if they are pretending to take our advice or just ignoring us after we leave. It does seem hopeless; these people are always playing the victim role. We cannot respond to this victim mentality.

Black People: Pastors are the instruments of the Presbytery to change us or to close the church. Why won't they listen to us? They just don't care or just don't get it.

Presbytery: Madrona is a troubled church that no one can ever lead effectively. Its members are not even honest. They must be mishandling money so we will take control of all their finances and transfer those funds to the Presbytery.

Interaction

White People: They are dishonest and are not to be trusted even with their own finances. They are not only incapable, they are thieves.

Black People: This is the final straw. The Presbytery has now taken total control over our church. They are not interested in us, they just want our money. \

Madrona: A complaint was filed with the Synod against the Presbytery. This complaint was done within the Book of Order and was appropriately filed. The ruling overturned the Presbytery and finances were returned to Madrona.

Interaction

Black People: They never apologized to us for accusing us of stealing money. In fact they charged a fee for managing our money.

White People: We have done what we can; we will take actions in the Presbytery that will control what they can do and we will simply move on.

Presbytery: There is an out-of-sight out-of-mind attitude beginning in the mid 1990's. Churches in the Presbytery form partnerships with Black non-Presbyterian congregations in Seattle. None do so with Madrona.

Madrona: Madrona received a new stated supply pastor they liked. Madrona went about its business without much contact with the Presbytery or other congregations. Madrona resented the lack of relationship with other churches in the Presbytery and felt regularly excluded.

Interaction

White People: At least they are not causing us a lot of problems. We will leave them alone. We don't need their victim attitude and manipulation. Just remember, Madrona is trouble.

Black People: They will never listen to us. They will only deny the truth and reject us. There is no point in making any attempts to relate to them. They want to close us and we will just have to wait until they try again. All of the other churches in the Presbytery are White and don't want anything to do with Blacks.

Presbytery: Finally Madrona is not the source of any problems and we are happy to leave them alone. Their stories are not believable and they use them only to manipulate others. If some of them appear at Presbytery meetings or serve on Presbytery committees we will be nice to them.

Madrona: Issues are reduced to relatively minor matters but each one carries an increased intensity. The strong belief that the Presbytery is trying to close them influences their responses to every decision and action by the Presbytery.

Presbytery: The good though naïve attempt at integration resulted in fifty years of increasing alienation.

Madrona: Integration felt like the old segregation. Madrona would not willingly comply with demands from the Presbytery ever again.

Interaction

White People: They are dishonest and are not to be trusted even with their own finances. They are not only incapable, they are thieves.

Black People: This is the final straw. They have now taken total control over our church. They are not interested in us, they just want our money.

Madrona: A complaint was filed with the Synod against the Presbytery. This complaint was done within the Book of Order and was appropriately filed. The ruling overturned the Presbytery and finances were returned to Madrona.

Interaction:

Black People: They never even apologized to us for accusing us of stealing money. In fact they charged a fee for managing our money.

White People: We have done what we can, we will take actions in the Presbytery that will control what they can do and we will simply move on.

Presbytery: There is an out-of-sight out-of-mind attitude beginning in the mid 1990's. Churches in the Presbytery form partnerships with Black non-Presbyterian congregations in Seattle. None do so with Madrona.

Madrona: Madrona receives a new stated supply pastor whom they like. Madrona went about its business without much contact with the Presbytery or other congregations. Madrona resented the lack of relationship with other churches in the Presbytery and felt regularly excluded.

Interaction:

White People: At least they are not causing us a lot of problems. We will leave them alone. We don't need their victim attitude and manipulation. Just remember, Madrona is trouble.

Black People: They will never listen to us. They will only deny the truth and reject us. There is no point in making any attempts to relate to them. They want to close our church; we will just have to wait until they try again. All of these other churches in the Presbytery are White and don't want anything to do with Blacks?

Presbytery: Finally Madrona is not the source of any problems and we are happy to leave them alone. Their stories are not believable and they use them only to manipulate others. If some of them appear at Presbytery meetings or serve on Presbytery committees we will be nice to them.

Madrona: Issues are reduced to relatively minor matters but each one carries an increased intensity. The strong belief that the Presbytery is trying to close them influences their responses to every decision and action by the Presbytery.

Presbytery: The good though naïve attempt at integration resulted in fifty years of increasing alienation.

Madrona: Integration felt like the old segregation. Madrona would not willingly comply with demands from the Presbytery ever again.

Systemic Racism

Organizations and institutions have racism embedded in their operating system and policies. The policies and procedures are designed to protect and preserve the organization or institution. It is also true that organizations and institutions set standards for behavior. There is always a correct way to do everything, and violation of these rules can mean expulsion. Organizations and Institutions are protectors of certain values and traditions. The great threat in organizations and institutions is the potential of losing control of the decision making process and thereby losing power. Great care is exercised in the process of developing and promoting new leaders. In the past and to some degree even now, people of different cultures and ethnic backgrounds need not apply. Clearly, this was involved in the "merger" between Grace and Madrona. If Madrona had acted like a White church, much of the problem would have gone away or may not have even occurred. Organizations and institutions are not monoliths. Every member of a White Church or a Black Church does not agree about everything. Every member of the Presbytery does not agree. Yet, when confrontation takes place and the spiral of reciprocal perceptions is at work, then we are inclined to make all inclusive statements like: "All Black people - " "Everyone at a meeting of the Presbytery thinks alike - " In times of less stress or conflict we can recognize such statements as being absurd. In conflict we will defend these absurd statements with great passion.

The spiral of reciprocal perception controlled the relationship between Madrona and Seattle Presbytery for a period of nearly fifty years.

CHAPTER EIGHT

Keys to Reconciliation

The Madrona experience taught us and continues to teach us that reconciliation is a fragile process over time. We can work very hard and suddenly feel it slip away if we do not continue to focus and maintain our determination. Reconciliation will not just happen. There is no magical or easy solution. Reconciliation seeks to resolve deep wounds and anger that have aged in dark isolation. Public racism remains hidden under a pretty veneer. Biases, stereotypes and prejudices have been built layer upon layer. As we dig through those layers, refined anger and fear confront us. Friendships become strained and old animosities reassert themselves.

There are requirements that we must meet if we intend to proceed in this quest. This is not a casual, accidental or unintentional process. Neither is it predictable, nor a planned step-by-step process. There is little we can control, nor can we produce an outline of goals and objectives. Reconciliation is a process that takes place in stages and each stage is essential to what follows. What happens in each stage and how it happens will depend upon what happened in the most immediate past. Failure to communicate and listen will prevent our ability to proceed.

We must back up and try again, and again, until we do communicate and listen. When we do communicate and listen, necessary next steps will be unclear. Breakthroughs will come in unexpected ways and at unexpected times and when they do we must pause and celebrate. We may never know why the breakthroughs occurred when they did. The process of reconciliation is ambiguous, and we must learn to be comfortable in ambiguity. This is a process that requires listening, not debating; receiving and not rejecting; caring for angry people and not denying the anger.

First, we commit ourselves to a long-term process, recognizing that it will be difficult and painful for us. We will hear stories that dismay us and devastate us. We will want to flee and avoid those stories but we must resolve not to flee or hide. We live in a society in which no one wants to take personal responsibility for any error or wrong. Reconciliation requires that we take responsibility for our own personal and corporate racism, face it, name it and refuse to let it control or influence our decisions and behavior. Without this commitment reconciliation cannot begin.

Second, we must know our history and our culture. We must be aware of the historical acts that reveal and expose the racism of our culture. Without this we can dismiss slavery as an issue in which we were not involved, resulting in our being blinded to the ongoing consequences of slavery. We have tried in the past to end racism without taking our culture into account and our efforts were doomed to failure. We must understand that racism is implanted in us by our culture. The lens through which we view the world has a distortion in it, and we must learn to adjust for that distortion and improve our vision.

When we have committed ourselves to a long painful process and have acknowledged the primary values of our culture, then we are ready to begin this improbable quest, a quest that our quest loving culture will resist. Cheering crowds and affirmation will not be forthcoming.

Relationship

"People of color often bite their tongues out of fear that, if they bring up race, they will be seen as "troublemakers" or "agitators" bent on fomenting "racial unrest."[36]African Americans and European Americans may know each other as acquaintances or even friends, but honest relationships are rare. Often those relationships ignore the elephant in the room and even depend upon maintaining that invisible elephant.

Honest relationships are crucial in our attempts to reconcile, yet that honesty is difficult to establish. White people cannot learn if the conversation is always polite and gentle because African Americans are reluctant to tell us how they feel or the experiences they have had, if they believe they will be rejected yet another time. African Americans and White Americans live separately most of the time. We may be colleagues at work but those settings are not commonly appropriate relationship building times. The work place has many rules about such matters. It is very unlikely that we attend the same churches or social events. Acquaintance is difficult to establish.

White people need to seek out opportunities for relationship building. We must seek out groups that are multicultural and multiethnic. We must extend ourselves to meet African Americans and to invite African Americans to enter our homes and communities. We must find ways to work against the social separation that continues even though segregation ended 50 years ago.

The necessity of this step brings us to reflect on our own feelings and reactions. Why would we resist visiting a Black church or joining a group that is majority Black? What do we fear? Why are we so sure that we will be uncomfortable? Do we fear being a minority in a group? What happens if a Black driver cuts us off on the freeway? How do we react when we hear Black parents complaining about the way their children are treated at school? Can we recall moments when we were confronted about our racism and denied it and avoided it? Our reticence to seek relationships with African Americans is the first indicator of our own racism. We must confess that racism to ourselves and explore experiences that have created it. Instead of letting guilt and shame immediately shout denial, we must allow ourselves to be honest with ourselves and with others.

As we are honest with ourselves we can begin to explore African American culture. We can begin reading history and learn the artists and heroes of that culture. We can ask an African American to tell us about Kwanzaa and its meanings. We can begin to learn African American culture instead of denying the existence of that culture. It will never be our culture, but we can appreciate its strengths and values.

If you have not had the experience of being a minority, seek out those opportunities. Seek situations where you will be the only White person in a large gathering. Reflect on your feelings and recognize that this is a common experience for African Americans. The warmth of welcome and hospitality may surprise you.

African Americans have lived within Northern European culture for centuries. They have learned how to survive in our context, but we have rarely entered their context and experienced their culture. They know how we work, but we know little of how they work. It is important that we learn their context and their culture if we ever expect to enter a reconciliation process.

If we are consistent in our acquaintances, we will find friendship and relationship. It is in this relationship that the possibility of reconciliation may emerge. We, as Northern Europeans, cannot create the confrontation nor should we try. Such an attempt will be artificial and dishonest. If we remain in a relationship for a period of time it is likely that we will do something or say something that will cause the confrontation to happen. We fear the confrontation and when it happens we want to control it. This desire to control situations is a primary way in which we act out our racism. Any initiative on our part to establish a relationship with African Americans will open the door to the confrontation which will be painful to us.

We must remember, however, that African Americans have learned to not bring up the race issue in casual social settings. They fear backlash and rejection. While this relationship is superficial we can remain open and responsive. This will provide some assurance that we will receive their anger. We must remain who we are, for our integrity and openness to difficult conversations will give permission to African Americans to be honest with us. Can we have a conversation with an African American who believes O.J. Simpson was framed and explore why they believe that? Can we do this and not become defensive if we believe he was guilty and got off because of his money?

Staying in the relationship over time is essential. In my own experience I stayed in relationship with Rudy Cuellar because I had little choice. I had been given an assignment and to some degree my job was dependent upon fulfilling it. In that case the relationship developed after the confrontation. Rudy confronted me the first time I met him and a year later we were becoming friends.

Reconciliation is not a recipe but it does have a lot to do with being available for the reconciliation process to begin.

We will never be a part of that process as long as we stay locked in our Whites only privileged and protected places. We must move out of our privilege and comfort zones. It is still possible in this country to live and work and never encounter or need or want a relationship with a person who is not White. Harlon Dalton in his book *Racial Healing: Confronting the Fear Between Whites and Blacks* tells a wonderful story about an experience at a Presbyterian Camp outside of Denver at Camp Insmont. It was especially fun for me as I had gone to that camp 10 years earlier than he had. He went with the first group of Black kids to attend that camp. The adults were obviously very anxious about the situation. One evening when they were singing around the campfire they sang the old camp song that took a word, that when divided made a noun and a verb. A little White girl finally came up with one after a long silence as everyone was trying to think of one. She said, "Have you ever seen a knee grow, a Negro?" The adults chastised her for insensitivity, while the Black kids thought it was funny and terrific. The importance of that story is that a relationship was about to bloom but was ended by the anxiety of White adult leaders. An opportunity was missed to start a reconciliation process. A commitment to become available, accessible and open to relationships with African Americans is the very first step in the reconciliation process.

Confrontation

The confrontation that takes place exposes our own racism. If we feel attacked or defensive and respond with denial the opportunity will vanish instantaneously. "When we truly commit ourselves to the conversation, we risk tapping into a storehouse of powerful feelings. Especially when we speak from the heart, we tap into anger and resentment that is difficult to modulate."[38] This fear on the part of African Americans is why they are reluctant to confront us in the first place. A response from us that is defensive will shut the door on the conversation. We must be willing to listen, not refute. We must listen to the anger recognizing that these are feelings that have built over a long period of time and are legitimate. We must respect those feelings and understand that those feelings have arisen from real events. We may have some experience with those events and see them very differently, but that does not discount the validity of the perspective or feelings being expressed. We must listen intently not to find ways to discredit those feelings or their perspective of those events. We must listen for the anger and ask to understand when we may have done the same things. It is never just about the past. The past has produced this outcome, but it is about us, not about those in the past. It is about understanding ourselves and our behaviors that continue the racism of the past into the future.

We must own the problem. This is not something that we can fix by changing African Americans and it is not something they can fix within us. They can and will forgive, but we own the problem. White people will often suggest that African Americans are racist against them. Somehow this is meant to justify our racism toward them. Whether they are or not is irrelevant. That is not our problem, nor is it a defense of our feelings. They cannot heal us of our racism and we cannot heal them of theirs if it exists. We each must own our problem. Any expectation that African Americans must do something for us to solve our problem is in itself a racist notion.

The events involving Madrona and Grace Churches were probably done for good and seemingly legitimate reasons. Given the era in which it took place, it was perhaps even courageous. What went wrong? The African Americans of Grace were not taken seriously, nor was either congregation aware of the cultural clash that was about to take place. Clearly there was a failure to understand African American culture, or perhaps there wasn't even recognition that such a culture existed. How often in our own time have we done exactly the same thing? Learning about the past is the way in which we learn about ourselves. If we apologize for the past, provide reparations and correct as well as we can the mistakes of the past and leave it there, nothing has actually changed. We will be doing things that require someone else 50 years from now to repent and apologize for. We cannot change the past but we can change in our present time. Change now will provide the foundation for a new future time.

Reconciliation will repeatedly lead us through that same thicket. Confrontations will continue as we work through this process. New events will raise old issues and we will need to listen carefully and respond with care. We will find ourselves working through this same difficult dynamic many more times.

Engagement

When Ivan and I were confronted by Daisy Dawson at Madrona that Saturday we had some options. We could claim no involvement as we were both relatively new in this Committee on Ministry role and thereby suggest this was not relevant to our task of the day. I do not know how they would have responded but there would have been no engagement.

We could have assured them that we had no such intention to close the church and that we were there to help them. Again, the outcome is unpredictable but we would have missed the opportunity to move toward reconciliation.

What we did do is nothing. We arranged for another meeting to listen. Engagement is not usually secured by

162

something we do, but probably more the result of something we don't do. We need to listen and turn off the denial and defense mechanisms. The important task for us in that moment was to engage the anger. We knew it would be painful and returning the next Saturday was not a pleasant prospect. "Insistence on pain-free engagement can be profoundly silencing for people who have difficult messages to deliver. It also provides a handy escape route for those who don't really want to engage anyway."[38]

I was influenced by conversations with a racially mixed group I had been a part of the last two years. This group had gathered after our first trip to South Africa. We had just finished a study of the book Divided by Faith and had discussed the feeling that racial healing seemed to be stuck in the United States and we weren't sure what to do about it. Those conversations had helped identify racism that lives undercover and unnamed in the United States. We had decided we would not continue to study racism nor adopt more resolutions denouncing it. We decided to name tasks that each member could complete, tasks that would overcome acts of racism. "If we are unhappy with the present state of race relations in America, then we ought to get together and do something about it. And it is high time we got started."[39] Perhaps that is why Ivan and I did mean it when we said, we needed more time for them to tell us the story. We recognized the pain in it and knew that we were launching a process that was likely to be filled with pain for a long time. We knew this would be an awkward and uncomfortable Saturday, but this congregation could not call a pastor and be an effective church if this story was not told. They could never provide effective ministry without a healing of the wounds and scars they carried. "We should relish these moments of extreme awkwardness and confusion, for they have the potential to teach us much about how race affects our lives, I speak with the zealousness of the convert."[39]

Reconciliation will never take place unless we are willing to engage each other across those racial lines. Engagement is more than listening, it is the commitment to be confronted and embrace the pain and hurt. We must embrace that which we have feared the most: the anger and the calling of us to account. Engagement is not warm and smooth, it is jagged and piercing. We want to let go of it. We can't let go of it; our commitment is to embrace it and take it into ourselves.

The two meetings that I had with the group that was unhappy about the Madrona video are instructive and illustrative. Though I agreed to listen and did so for two hours, there was no engagement. I had hoped that after the first meeting the anger would be vented enough that we could engage in the second meeting. Again there was no engagement. They could not listen, nor could they engage the pain and anger of the Madrona people. There was no dialogue, there were lectures and presentations detailing my failure to understand that I had been conned by people who want to be victims.

This is the typical reaction when we are confronted by our own racism. We deny, we defend, and we fill silence with meaningless words all of which silence the voice of the African Americans. If they do not respond we declare victory and go on about our business. If they do respond they will need to do so assertively and with emotion which allows us to declare them to be irrational. Our dismissal of them is quick and complete. Once again we have been vindicated and we go on about our business. Amazingly we are puzzled by the anger that we sense in African Americans. I am puzzled by their patience and willingness to forgive.

My intent had been to begin the process of reconciliation between the people of Madrona and these very angry members of the Presbytery. Lacking engagement reconciliation did not happen and still has not happened.

Response – Commitment to Reconciliation

I am not sure anything is as counterintuitive to the culture of King Arthur as repentance and apology. The culture of Arthur is built on the assumption that we are right, we know best and when others learn to be like us they will be okay. We are more likely to expect they will apologize to us for suggesting that we have done something wrong. There is a persistent voice in our culture that assures us we were right, and they were wrong in not seizing the opportunity we gave them. There is an insidious ability to rationalize our conquest instincts. If our denial does not work, we default to "we did it for their own good." They somehow failed, they somehow messed it up. Our racism takes over and again asserts that something is just wrong with them because they just can't ever seem to get it right.

When we engage, we embrace the pain that we have caused and that we see and hear. We always have two choices: we can claim unjustified pain and walk away or we can apologize and seek forgiveness. However, the apology can be very hollow. We can apologize in our time and on our terms. We can design and plan the apology. We can control all aspects of our apology and put our spin on it. The apology can become a quid pro quo, and we again are the winners. Even our apology can be disingenuous.

We must learn when we engage that only those who have been damaged by our behavior have the power to forgive. We do not have that power as the perpetrators, only the victims do. Recognizing our powerlessness is counter to the very central assertion of our culture. If we are to apologize, repent and seek forgiveness we must be on their turf in a service designed by them and controlled by them. Equally discomfiting for us is the realization that our apology does not necessarily mean they will forgive. This is their option; they may or may not forgive. What if we participate in a service of apology and repentance and at the conclusion they announce that they do not forgive us? What then? We still have two choices, we can disengage and live in racial alienation as we have, or continue to be engaged to understand why they do not forgive us. Reconciliation is hard work.

The Madrona session set the date of the service of repentance and apology for the first Sunday in October, 2003. The service would be at Madrona and the pastor and session would plan the service. We were asked to send them a statement of apology and repentance that would be included in the bulletin and which I would read.

We did not see the bulletin until we arrived for the service. The sanctuary was filled with people from Madrona and the Presbytery. African American symbols and traditions set the framework. The Kenyan Choir sang and there was a spirit of joy and celebration. Dale Sewall offered a powerful statement of the benefits received by Mercer Island at the expense of Madrona. I read the statement of apology. There was more I wanted to say, but I had said what needed to be said. I sat down with a feeling of relief and expectation.

The question of whether they would accept the apology was a real question. I thought they would; it is one of the gifts they have to give us. They are forgiving people. However, I had seen the anger and deep hurt; perhaps they would not be ready to take that step. The service bulletin declared forgiveness but still I wondered. It was a powerful moment for us when they said they did indeed forgive us. It was one of those very special moments, a taste that we wanted to experience again. The service was powerful and astonishing.

At the end of that service of apology and repentance, the next question quickly arose. We had healed the past and were reconciled. Or were we? What would it mean the next day? Would we go about our business as usual, happy that we had conquered another problem? How would we live out the reconciliation? How would we learn to not repeat the past?

As we were raising that question about ourselves, we were surprised that so were the people of Madrona. The service had opened a door to a new relationship and healing, but none of us were clear about what that meant. One thing it meant was the remodeling of a building and as important as that would be, it didn't address the relationships between people. How do we work together and learn together to fulfill the commitment we made in this worship experience?

Very soon we experienced incidents that required us to live as reconciled people. Those situations would have been far easier to resolve prior to the service of apology. We could have just told everyone what to do and move on. We wouldn't have had to talk carefully with each other about how we would work through those issues and problems. As we did so we got a glimpse of what we can do together, but it was still very new and we were all very tentative.

We must continue our commitment to reconciliation, we must continue to be engaged and sit in awkward relationships. We yearn for comfort and ease in all of this, but we keep hearing "not yet." There continue to be people in Mercer Island Presbyterian Church and Seattle Presbytery who refuse to engage in reconciliation. We continue to explain and converse, but still there are those voices that refuse to enter the conversation. As I have said before, reconciliation is very hard work.

Reconciled Relationships, Mutual Respect and Candid Dialogue

"When we surface our racial misgivings and candidly explore the ways in which they influence our policy preferences, we just might get unstuck. We would spend less time searching for double meanings and hidden agendas, and would be much less likely to miscalculate each others intentions. And we would be in a much better position to design and pursue win-win solutions."[41]

We can recognize and change institutional racism. Together we can confront racial profiling, imprisonment of young Black males, and economic disparity. We can identify White privilege and the disadvantage faced by African Americans. We can begin to dismantle racism in our society. This improbable quest will lead us to that goal, indeed a holy grail. In South Africa they affirm that they must learn to recognize racism and name it every time they see it. If they can do that, they believe they can stop racism from influencing their decisions and actions. They further affirm that if they can do that, then perhaps their grandchildren will not live in a racist society. I hope they are right and I hope someday, someone will write about the successful completion of this quest in the United States. My grandchildren are adolescents and the youngest is two years old. Perhaps one of their children will be able to write that story.

Summary of Necessary Steps

The Steps of Preparation for White People

Learn your culture. Identify the racism embedded in it and the ways you express that racism. "The basic propositions about the centrality of race and the superiority of Whites pervade interactions in our culture, and institutional forms make those theses part of everyday experience."[42]

Confront racism in yourself. This may require relationships with African Americans who can point it out to you. When this happens, receive and reflect upon it. We in the general European American public share many beliefs with the militant White racists, but we are not identical to them – it is **not** that "we met the enemy, and he is us." "We Whites believe many things; we believe most them in a dull and muddled and jumbled fashion; many of our beliefs are contradictory."[43]

Recognize the spiral of reciprocal perceptions and learn to recognize when that spiral is happening. Listen for it in your conversations. Learn to step out of it, learn to stop it and better yet, learn to not enter it.

Learn your role in that spiral. Listen and receive rather than responding defensively. "Most White Americans, however, have little acquaintance with the parts of their psyches that are congruent with the spirit of the acknowledged racists. We do not know, the old joke says, who discovered the water, but we do know that it was not a fish. Just so, in a society in which White folk predominate and are seldom challenged in everyday life, White Americans have little conscious awareness of being White or of what that might mean. Only challenge or crisis makes this categorization relevant. The militant

White racist movement is composed of people who permanently feel in crisis."[44]

Listen for the pain, hurt and anger rather than arguing with details of stories or denying your role in the events being described. The event itself may have taken place long ago and you were not involved. Yet, the event took place, the hurt is present, and the continuing racism makes us all complicit in it.

Learn to explore those events by asking for more information in order to learn the depth of pain, hurt and anger being expressed. Seek historical resources and books about racism.

Prepare yourself that you are not able to fix the event or the pain, hurt and anger. Prepare yourself to be vulnerable in finding ways to apologize, seek forgiveness and work toward reconciliation. This process necessarily is one in which African Americans are invited to point out our racism whenever they see it or hear it. It is at that point that we learn to recognize racism and refuse to act on the basis of it.

Identify White privilege and the ways in which it has benefited you. I worked my way through college as a night mechanic in a bowling alley. As long as the machines ran properly I could study. I actually got paid while studying. I also delivered mail on Saturdays and during the Christmas rush. I worked 60 hours a week and went to college. We were married and had a son. So, where is the privilege in that? It was that I could get two jobs in a small Missouri community while a Black student who lived in the African American part of town had to quit college because he could not afford the costs. This Black student and I had taken some classes together. We knew each other as little more than acquaintances. I didn't know why he had dropped out until much later. The demonic part of White privilege is that White people are unaware of the privilege and Black people live resentfully in the midst of it every day of their lives.

Preparation for African Americans

It is preposterous to suggest that burden of ending racism be placed on the backs of African Americans. We have asked them to tell us their story and then we have ignored it or responded in platitudinous ways. I cannot ask African Americans to do this, nor can I offer directives that will make this issue more palatable to White people. I do have a suggestion, however. The statement made by Daisy Dawson was clear, precise, blunt and articulate. There were no details or lengthy explanations. We heard her, because she stated it without details. The details can be a source of argument and distraction which provide the opportunity for White people to deflect the pain, hurt and anger. There is ample opportunity to explore all the details, but those details are not the issue. Engaging each other without entering the spiral of reciprocal perceptions is the pathway to understand and to heal. We cannot ask you as African Americans to be patient with us; you have already been patient for a very long time. The burden is ours and the problem is ours.

CHAPTER NINE

The Church: Racism and Reconciliation

Are we agents for change or unwitting co-conspirators?

It is not coincidental that "White Anglo Saxon Protestant" is the label attached to the privileged portion of the population in the United States. Northern Europeans migrated to the new world and after a revolution established a new nation. That new nation was a radical political departure from the Old World, but came from the same cultural perspective as the Old World. They were on a quest. They wrote documents of freedom for themselves but held slaves. They established a democracy giving the right to vote and elect leaders provided the voter was male and owned land. The culture was exported in its totality to this new world and new nation.

These same people formed churches. Religious freedom was one of their primary issues. It is not surprising that the church carried those same core values and identities as the culture at large. How could we expect anything different? Today their descendants continue to be the majority in the traditional mainline denominations. As people enter the church on a Sunday morning their culture is not removed, the culture enters with them. This is true for the church in every culture. Indigenous Presbyterian Churches around the world are not clones of the Presbyterian Church in the United States. Attempts in the late 1890's to evangelize the world implanted the culture of the United States and Western Europe in these new churches. Today, those same churches have recovered and continue to recover their own culture and are increasingly distinct from the culture of the missionaries. They each are shaped by the culture of the people who attend them and lead them. The Book of Order of the Presbyterian Church in Cameroon, West Africa is about four pieces of single fold legal sized paper. The index of the Book of Order of the Presbyterian Church (USA) requires more paper than that.

Earlier we talked about culture as the lens through which we see reality. We read scripture through that same lens. Those portions of scripture that our culture does not understand are difficult for us to process. For example, we are all of us the wealthiest people on this planet, no matter our income. From a global perspective we are the rich that Jesus refers to when he says it is easier for a camel to get through the eye of a needle than for a rich man to enter the kingdom of heaven. The materialism of our culture blinks and either passes it by or offers a more amenable interpretation.

The church has stood for justice, peace and social righteousness. We have stood on some difficult battle lines to bring the values of the gospel to this society. The Presbyterian Church, as many other denominations, was split over the issue of slavery. We stood valiantly in the Civil Rights Movement of the 1960s. We have stood with farm workers. During the grape boycott in California I came to understand the geography of this work. It was easier for Northerners to stand for civil rights in the South than in the North. It was easier for those in cities to stand with the farm workers than those who lived in farming regions. Similarly the stand for peace tends to be more difficult in areas where there is a strong military presence.

Many have worked hard on these and many other issues for a long time. Consistently, however, we have not dealt with our culture. We have not worked to understand the counter cultural role of the gospel nor acted in those ways. We have been slow to acknowledge our culture and the ways it informs our life in the church. There have been times we have dreamed of being the church that can live in this culture but not be of it. Ironically, some who have attempted to do so became cults that resulted in destructive aberrations.

We continue to build opulent churches that I fear signal to poor people and people of color that they are not welcome. One day I was walking from the parking lot of a church outside of Fresno on my way to a meeting of ethnic commissioned lay pastors. I met one of the Latino lay pastors as we approached the church. As we walked toward the sanctuary door, he stopped and said "This is very strange." I asked him why it was so strange. "I was raised in this community. My parents were farm workers here. I was told to never go into this church because it was the church of the patrons."

We cannot be surprised that our church functions by the same cultural norms and patterns that we have observed throughout this conversation. We cannot be surprised that our systems of decision making reflect those core values. We cannot be surprised though we may deny that our systems and structures exclude people the same way our culture does. Two hundred years later the Presbyterian Church is still 95 percent White. We need no other evidence to convince us that everything we have discussed here regarding racism in our culture is true for the same reasons and in the same way in the Presbyterian Church (USA).

It is not that we have ignored the issue. We have studied racism, drafted resolutions denouncing racism, we have developed projects to end racism and we have done so for a very long time. We argue that progress has been made, which is true. Jim Crow Laws and enforced segregation have ended, yet the problem persists. We cannot attempt to hide behind the limited progress made in 50 years when we see even those gains being eroded. Can we identify in our structure and process why all of that effort over an extended period of time has not ended racism within the Presbyterian Church or the society at large?

An examination of some recent attempts may help us understand our failure. Presbyterian Women recognized that they needed to address the issue of racism and inclusion. "At its 1997 Church-wide Business Meeting, Presbyterian Women approved a resolution to seek to eradicate racism."[45] The acknowledgment of the problem is always the first step. During the next three years the church-wide coordinating team participated in antiracism events and training. There was affirmation that anyone participating in antiracism activities must first acknowledge their own racism and participation in it. These beginning steps are positive examples of confronting the issue. We can however, begin to see an underlying problem. A group of leaders within Presbyterian Women participated and made these affirmations. Presbyterian Women across the church did not participate nor did they make those same affirmations. The voting representatives did however act in 2000 to adopt an "antiracism identity." The Church-wide Coordinating Committee was directed to appoint a task group to review the entire organization from an antiracism perspective. This is an admirable policy and direction, but we must ask the obvious question. Can a small representative group of leaders change the racism within an entire national organization? The answer is no. The vast majority of the members and local organizations did not confront this reality in a personal way unless by their own initiative. Given the difficulty of this issue, it is doubtful that this spread through significant numbers of people.

The Structural Review Task Group was balanced and included diverse cultural and racial groups. Again, this is commendable. However, the primary problem is not addressed by this inclusive strategy. The phrase "preaching to the choir" applies. An extensive survey was conducted as part of this review process. The major findings of this survey confirm the problem. The report begins with the observation of the critical problem in dealing with racism.

> *"The results indicate that in general all Presbyterian Women leaders value the contributions of women from many racial ethnic backgrounds and agreeing that Presbyterian Women is strengthened by this richness. Additionally, there is lack of agreement on the existence of racism."*[46]

At the outset of this commendable effort, the organization does not agree on the most basic level. The national organization is standing against racism while there is no agreement that racism even exists.

Given this information we should not be surprised that "all racial ethnic groups, except European Americans, had many leaders identify changes in communication patterns as important to creating a more inclusive and caring community."[47] The Arthurian cultural pattern is clearly and dominantly in place. The failure to understand this cultural response is crippling to the process. Those same Northern Europeans most likely are those who do not believe racism exists. I will say it again: we must first learn our own culture, recognize the racism of that culture and acknowledge our own racism, so we are able to confront that in each other. Until we do so, there is little basis upon which to proceed.

This is demonstrated by a very significant disconnect in communication that was discovered by the Task Group in their survey. "All racial ethnic leaders, except for the European American women, emphasized the importance of being sensitive to a variety of ways of processing ideas."[48] The ability to communicate requires awareness of the perceptions and perspectives of others. Perhaps we can recognize differences in decision making with African Americans if we recognize this same difficulty persists in multicultural settings as well.

Northern Europeans tend to formalize group decision making processes. Rules of debate are imposed and carefully monitored. Robert's Rules of Order is the nearly universal guide. Decision making is a primarily political process that ends with voting on a motion. The winning side needs only one more vote than the losing side. The debate process is the opportunity for each side to gain at least that one vote. Presbyterians in particular pride themselves on doing everything decently and in order. Debate of very controversial issues is often not very exciting. Speeches may be impassioned, but by the rules are always decorous.

The lack of personal relationships is a common concern and frequent complaint in presbyteries of the Presbyterian Church USA). Indeed this decision making process can and often does take place among total strangers. Ideas are being debated, not people. The debate may strain the social courtesies but it does not increase or decrease the shallowness of relationships. As a result of the debate both sides will build a case for why the other side voted as they did. The generalizations and biases become the basis for like minded group formation. The longer the debate the more rigid and narrowly defined those groups become. Remember the Knights of the Round Table were a group of individuals; they were not a community, nor did their identity or life depend upon relationships with each other. They all went on their own quests, returning to the Round Table once a year to share and celebrate their adventures.

People from cultures other than Northern European are almost immediately bewildered when they attend one of our meetings. We gather, we read minutes, approve the docket and start our decision making process. Relational cultures, familial cultures cannot start a meeting until the relationships have all been renewed and updated. Decisions are made relationally, and without renewal of those relationships a decision cannot be made.

This story illustrates the difference. It was time to review the study outlines for Commissioned Lay Pastors who may serve as pastors without seminary education in the Presbyterian Church (USA). This is a particularly helpful provision for new immigrant fellowships. The Lay Ministry Committee represented eight cultures and six language groups. Consuelo Donahue, a Colombian woman, was the chair of the committee. Members of the committee were Indonesian, Mexican, Vietnamese, Cambodian, African American and Bolivian. They came from Las Vegas, Fresno, Bakersfield, Modesto, Stockton and Sacramento. Airline schedules were such that our time to meet would be limited to 10:00am to 2:00pm on a Saturday, and the easiest location was our office in Sacramento. In this particular meeting we would need to outline the studies for the Old and New Testaments. It seemed unlikely to me that we could get all of that work done in four hours, but we always have to work within limits, so I agreed.

On the appointed day I arrived at the office at 9:15 in the morning. Being the dutiful Northern European compulsive staff person, I made coffee, laid out papers, set up the projection equipment, etc. At ten o'clock all was ready to go. There was a problem, however. I was still alone in the building. Members of the committee began arriving at 10:15 and at 10:30 all were present. My anxiety had already gone up a few degrees. We had lost thirty minutes of an already very limited amount of time.

As is the cultural norm for most people on this planet, except Northern European compulsive people, there is a need to connect personally before business is conducted. For many cultures business cannot be conducted outside of personal relationships that are well intact and renewed. So, everyone began sharing stories of family, ministry and general life experiences. While I found this quite enjoyable, my sense of time kept raising my anxiety. Soon it was 11:00 and then 11:30. Still the chair had made no move to start the meeting.

To my dismay, at 11:45, Consuelo calmly announced that since it was so close to noon, perhaps we should take a break and have lunch. Somewhere deep inside me was a voice shouting, "BREAK? WHAT BREAK? WE HAVEN'T EVEN STARTED YET!!"

"Well," I said to myself. "So much for this project. We can't possibly finish. The Kingdom of God will be denied, the world will end, nothing is possible, and we missed another deadline." Having come to this conclusion I had an enjoyable lunch sharing in the continuing conversations. After all, this wouldn't be my first failure in multiethnic-multicultural ministry and probably wouldn't be my last.

At about one o'clock Consuelo said, "Well, perhaps we should get started." This struck me as a rather pointless idea, but, hey, whatever works. To my absolute amazement the group discussed the Old Testament issues, and all agreed that Genesis, Exodus, Joshua, Samuel and the Psalms were essential. Francisco wanted Amos and Jeremiah as prophets, but Phebe an Indonesian pastor wanted Isaiah. They agreed that it would be fine to have Amos and Isaiah. They then did a brief outline of themes and content. At 1:30 they began to discuss the New Testament. Francisco felt Matthew and Romans were crucial, Phebe felt that Luke Acts and Ephesians would be better. They concluded that Luke, Acts, Romans and Ephesians would be a good introductory outline. They again did a brief outline of themes and content. At 1:55 Consuelo handed me the rather impressive stack of paper, and asked if there was anything else they needed to do. Still somewhat dazed by what I had just witnessed, I said no. They closed with prayer, and we all said our good-byes and they left.

I realized that due to no help from me, they had accomplished an amazing amount of work in what appeared to be a short period of time. I finally realized that they had been discussing these issues all morning, had actually worked out their disagreements, and understood why some choices were so important to some cultural groups. All they needed to do was meeting formally to confirm what they had informally decided. This was my first full introductory course in multiethnic decision making. I learned a lot. I left our office wondering if I could figure out a way for them to plan Presbytery meetings.

It is this reality that the non Northern Europeans in the Presbyterian Women's study were demanding. Perception of reality and decision making processes is one of the primary obstacles to overcome if we intend to seek reconciliation. We must learn that African Americans and most other cultures do not perceive a reality in the same way as Northern Europeans. The Arthurian Culture is convinced that there is one correct way to do business and to process information. We continue in the attempt to train people to do it our way and don't understand why they won't or can't comply.

We can anticipate the next level of problem identified in this report.

"Over 50 percent of the racial ethnic leaders, except for the European American women, identified a lack of willingness to change as barriers to inclusive and caring community. When this is examined in relation to the comments about what helps to create community, this may refer to the behavior of the European American Presbyterian Women groups."[49]

It is about our acts and the ways in which we behave. Due to our own lack of awareness, our behavior is informed by our racism. Those who are not Northern Europeans clearly see it. What are they to think of our motives? We say one thing, but behave in an entirely different way. Do we expect people to accept our goodwill while our behavior remains the same? Certainly we have learned that our words carry meaning only when they reflect our behavior. We seem to know this fact as the church and we know it as individual Christians, except when the topic is racism.

The good news is that Presbyterian Women leadership and representatives recognized the problem and even named it. However, the attempt to resolve the matter had fundamental flaws. This was not a dialogue in a multicultural setting in which all people's shared equal voice and power. This was Northern Europeans talking to each other about ways to include people who were not present. There wasn't even agreement that racism exists. Where was the wide spread engagement? Where was the acknowledgement of the consequences of racism? Where was the repentance and apology? Where was the hard work of reconciliation taking place? Perhaps this happened in the leadership and some representatives, but certainly not in the whole organization.

There is a lesson in this for us all. We can confront the issue of racism theoretically, but we have great difficulty being confronted by and engaged with the people who are the victims of our racism. In fact, our very structure and polity seems to be part of the problem. Our polity is representative in nature and assumes that actions taken by representatives will be followed as mandates for change. Our polity only includes those within the organization. Those who need to confront us and with whom we must engage are not present. Consequently, Northern Europeans talk theoretically about racism and adopt very well crafted policy statements but the behavior continues to be offensive to those outside. How can we expect that they would be likely to come into the church?

Another instance of this failure took place at the 2003 Pre-Assembly Conference of the General Assembly which focused on antiracism resources. Commissioners to the 113th General Assembly gathered in the Kentucky International Convention Center on June 9 for a "special pre-Assembly event" during which they were challenged to "affirm that racism is a sin, a violation of God's intent for his people," and to work for its elimination as "a matter of discipleship."[50] This call was another good attempt to name the problem and confront it. Again, the same problems persisted. These were Northern Europeans talking to each other and most were far from home. Victims of racism were not there in equal number, power and voice.

This may point to a very real structural problem. For such a conversation to actually have impact, it would require that the near the majority in the room be people who experience our racism. They need to be there with equal voice and power. The conversation must be held within relationships that candidly and openly address racism and the way it works. We cannot have that conversation by ourselves within our own institutions and expect a different outcome. This is a major hurdle for the Presbyterian Church (USA) to overcome.

Here is one more example for our reflection. In 1995, the Presbyterian Church committed itself to having ten percent of its membership ethnic minority by the year 2010. A small step indeed to create the above mentioned ideal setting. This was a wonderful policy statement, but the effort was never funded. Further, to this date there has been no discussion regarding the profound system changes that must be made in the attempt to reach ethnic people, let alone if we were somehow to succeed in the goal. We have continued to make the assumption that those who will become part of us will become like us and will then be okay. We will change very little in order to receive people from different cultures; they must change to fit our systems and needs. This problem persists in Seattle Presbytery even though we have worked at reconciliation and do so at a very personal level. The unbalanced power between a Northern European Presbytery and a small number of African Americans has not been solved. Increasing participation by a wide variety of new ethnic communities is helping, but this is a slow process as well. Seattle Presbytery may have an advantage in that discussion as we continue to build healthy and reconciled relationships with the members of Madrona. Good intentions, however, will not suffice. The reconciliation process continues to confront us with challenge and we must continue to work faithfully with each other. Perhaps someday we will find that new community in Seattle Presbytery.

The book *Divided By Faith* states this issue in very helpful terms. "This book is a story of how well-intentioned people, their core values, and their institutions actually recreate racial divisions and inequalities they ostensibly oppose. It is a narrative of how some of America's core values and assumptions and its reliance on market principles contradict and work against other esteemed values."[51]

We have not considered the power of the gifts that new communities of people might bring us. New insights of faith, ministry and social change that could be brought to us to widen the diversity are dismissed as having no value and are lost. They must leave those gifts at the door of the church as they affirm that we are right and know best and therefore do not need their gifts. King Arthur was pretty much convinced of the same thing.

It is striking to place the church alongside the obvious perspective of Scripture. Throughout scripture there is a common theme. That theme begins in Genesis with Cain and Abel. Cain killed Abel, was banished and went to the Land of Nod, east of Eden. One of my youthful puzzlements was to figure out how Adam and Eve had two sons and were the source of all human life. A son and daughter would work biologically, but that would suggest a questionable moral beginning of the human race. Of course the problem was solved by racial intermarriage with the people of Nod. But where did they come from if Adam and Eve are the first human beings? This story and tradition was about Hebrew beginnings. There were others already in the neighborhood. Cain, who had committed murder, married someone from Nod, a Nodish or Nodder. I don't know what they might have called themselves.

Later the Hebrews believed that faithfulness to the covenant required separation from everyone else. However, in the very earliest stories of the Bible racial and cultural intermingling took place. In fact, this theme continues throughout the Scripture. Joseph was sold into slavery by his brothers, became a high official in the Egyptian court and provided the food for his family that saved them in a time of famine. Moses, a Hebrew raised as an Egyptian, led the Hebrews out of Egypt in the central event of all Judaism. Cyrus, the Persian, released the Hebrew exiles from captivity so they could return and rebuild the temple. On at least three occasions the Hebrews were saved by another culture, even an enemy culture.

In the Gospels, Jesus seems intent upon breaking the narrow cultural and racial convictions held by the Jews of his day. The story of the woman at the well, the Good Samaritan, and the repeated references to the coming of the Kingdom of God when all people will stream to Jerusalem are examples. The ending of the Gospel of Matthew with the Great Commission and the Great Commandment stated by Jesus earlier in the Gospel are clear: all people are our neighbors and all receive grace.

Peter was taught that lesson dramatically in Acts 10. Paul reasserts it over and over again. The church is to go into the world and share the gospel. There are no Jews or Greeks, slave or free, male or female in the church. All are one and all are received equally.

Yet, we see, that though the 1818 Presbyterian General Assembly said slavery was "utterly inconsistent with the Law of God," they also were sympathetic to slaveholders, whom they perceived to be trapped in a moral dilemma (and who were indeed caught in a moral dilemma of their own making), "Thus, they recommended that slave owners support the colonization society, give religious instruction, and, to the degree possible, avoid cruel treatment of slaves. At this very same assembly, a decision was also upheld to dispose of a Presbyterian minister due to his antislavery views, largely because they were deemed too radical."[52] The only change in that ambivalence and hypocrisy is that we no longer have the institution of slavery. In our time it has become subtle, hidden beneath piles of anti racism rhetoric.

For the better part of two millenniums, the people of the church resided in various places around the world but lived in isolation from each other. Churches grew as mono-cultural entities because there was only one culture around them. Churches developed systems, ideas and theology that were shaped by that culture. It is understandable that prior to the exploration of the world, the church was culture bound. It is equally understandable that during colonization the church remained cultural bound; colonies were extensions not new creations. It was not until the late Nineteenth Century that people from different cultures immigrated to the United States and begin living as neighbors. It is not surprising that it took several decades before the Swedish, Dutch, Norwegians, Irish, Scots, English and others finally gave up their national roots as the definition of their church. The Melting Pot myth was born. Finally language and customs gave way to a homogenized White culture. They were all from the same culture and perceived reality in the same ways. Realizing the difficulty for White cultures to come together, imagine the much greater difficulty between Whites and people of color, between cultures that do not perceive reality in the same way.

Consequently, Sunday morning continues to be the most segregated hour in this country. How do we explain that without naming the racism that is systemic in our church? How do we ignore the common theme of Scripture that the church is for all people? How do we ignore the clear vision that the church is to be multicultural and multiethnic?

I was attracted to scuba diving by the incredible diversity of interdependent life that fills coral reefs. There is a complex symbiotic relationship between every living thing.

I especially enjoyed watching cleaning stations. Large fish would literally line up and wait their turn. They would come to a particular place on the reef where small wrasse would clean their gills and mouths. Those parasites left unattended would threaten the fish's life but were food for the wrasse. The wrasse could have been food for the large fish, but were perfectly safe. The large fish would open their gills and mouths as the wrasse scurried in and out.

I was usually content to dive a reef, hold the depth and watch. I didn't dive because I loved diving; I did it because I loved to watch the life on reefs. Each time I watched I realized the God of all creation really likes diversity. It would be hard to imagine all of the shapes, sizes and colors of a creature that has two eyes, a head, a tail and gills. At least I think they all had two eyes. Not only was the diversity amazing to watch, the community relationships were unbelievable. There were many inhabitants of the reef that you could see only at night. The day belonged to some and the night belonged to others. Teeming life all needing each other and in their diversity bringing to the reef the resources for the survival of the reef.

I liked to watch reefs because the interdependence of creation was so easy to see there. The same thing is true on land, but it is much harder to see and human beings have not figured out how to do it yet. It always seemed to me that God's will for creation is seen on a reef at 50 to 80 feet under water.

We have been reconciled with God, and have received the means to reconcile with each other. God has called us to be those who reconcile and bring that message of grace to the world. The mandate or charter of the church is clear in II Corinthians 5:16-21. We are to be the agents of reconciliation. From the moment we are reconciled with God, the old has passed away and the new has come. We are called as reconciled people to be reconciling people. We have heard these words and repeated those words hundreds of times on Sunday mornings. We leave on Sunday mornings and enter an alienated world and feel overwhelmed. We wait for someone to do something, refusing to believe that we are the ones. We rationalize and make excuses and finally convince ourselves that hatred and alienation are decreasing. We decide it is better to do nothing rather than risk making it worse. The words we uttered and heard Sunday morning ring hollow. "Because reality is socially (in my view culturally) constructed, a highly effective way to ensure the perpetuation of a racialized system is simply to deny its existence. Contemporaries are not doing this out of some old form of Jim Crow racism, but based on their cultural tools and relative isolation." [53]

The lie of our rationalizations is exposed when we see economic inequality, racial profiling, white privilege, the disproportionate imprisonment of young Black men and crosses burned in the yards of Black families. Our denial of White privilege and defense of racial profiling as a valid tool of law enforcement exposes the lie we tell ourselves. God must certainly weep for the church.

When we consider the keys to reconciliation and recognize the pain and difficulty of reconciliation, one must wonder whether the church has trivialized it into handshakes and smiles all around. Have we taken the free gift of grace and cheapened reconciliation in the process?

Why we are as we are is a result of the culture that we share. We live in our culture as we seek to be faithful to our Lord. We have grown so accustomed to the culture that lives within us we forget it is even there. It directs us even when we think it is not directing us. The gospel lives in us as well. However, the gospel lives within the culture and while it tries to hold the culture accountable, we have difficulty hearing that gospel over the protests of our culture.

Racism is sin and is blasphemy. Racism denies the reconciliation that God has given. For us to tell people that racism is immoral provides little help in understanding it, naming it, and refusing to be influenced by it. The church must learn to address racism in culture for it is also the culture of the church. We must change our systems and learn to name racism every time we see it in our systems. We must begin to build relationships in which the confrontation can take place and we can engage. When that happens the church will have the opportunity to find new health and life and become what it was called to be. Until then we have a frightening similarity to whitened sepulchers.

Some years ago I attempted to describe these cultural interchanges and dynamics. I wanted to find a way to visualize it. I offer it now hoping that it may provide another way to think about the task before us.

The Fluid Sculpture

A gigantic, many faceted sculpture is being viewed from many angles by encircling clusters of individuals. The sculpture is so large that the viewers are often separated by great distance. The sculpture has a fluid quality. It appears solid, but its appearance changes. Not only does it look quite different from various angles, but it subtly changes while being viewed from one constant perspective. This sculpture incorporates many different and complex scenes and symbols. These numerous elements cause persons viewing from the same perspective to disagree as to its meaning and content. Yet, each cluster of viewers has some generalized convictions about what it represents. No one seems quite sure why, but each cluster of persons views the sculpture while standing in a cubicle. Their vision to the right and left of the circle is impaired and often blocked. While nothing prevents persons from leaving their cubicle and going to another, few do. The majority of those that do, do so for brief intervals only. Until recently few have moved to another cubicle for extended periods of time.

Each cluster of viewers tends to believe that their view is the best view of the sculpture, and feel most comfortable viewing the sculpture from their familiar vantage point. Some clusters of viewers have periodically attempted to force other clusters to see the sculpture as they do, but such attempts have only resulted in a distorted and manipulated view of the sculpture. At times these encroachments have resulted in violence.

While it is possible for the clusters of viewers to compare and contrast their views and thereby gain a more holistic view of the sculpture, few attempts have been made to do so. There is resistance in most of the clusters to such an idea, as these other perspectives raise troubling questions and challenge their own view as being the correct and valid perspective.

Some have suggested that their perspective is obviously the dominant view and have sought to assimilate all others into that perspective. Of course, such an attempt would mean that other clusters of viewers would have to give up their perspective and adopt that of the presumed dominant group. Most seem content to let each group have their own perspective and continue in relative isolation.

A few seek the opportunity to observe the whole sculpture. They want to understand it as a whole. These persons have suggested that the clusters of viewers must learn to share their unique perspectives with each other. Persons must begin to move in and out of each other's cubicles learning the perspective of each cubicle. Recently the pressure for such interchange has increased dramatically. Now, many people are taking up residence in cubicles other than their cubicle of origin. Now, people are hearing and witnessing the variety of ways in which the sculpture is viewed. Some react to these new intruders with hatred and suspicion, others try to ignore them. Some recognize the value of gaining a perspective of the whole sculpture, and thus experience and know more of what is true.

The ability to move between clusters requires specific relational skills. Customs acceptable in one cubicle are offensive to those in another. Sometimes these customs are easily identifiable, and other times are very subtle. Since this kind of exchange has been rare, it is difficult to describe and define those skills. Certainly sensitivity, ability to listen, and intentional observation are some of them. The different languages of the cubicles make this even more difficult. Each cubicle has exclusively taught its own language, and multilingual people are more and more prized.

This becomes very complex. Each cubicle resident must teach and learn symbols, values and perspectives of their own cubicle and those of others. Each cubicle of viewers must learn skills to see the sculpture from that new perspective. But, each cluster of viewers also must understand their own perspective and be open to receive one that is different. Few have even attempted such an ambitious project.

All of this is made more complex by the history of relationships between some of the cubicle residents. In the past they have disparaged each other, attacked each other, and have even killed each other. The trust necessary for this task of sharing is very weak, and in some cases doesn't exist at all.

The recent significant movement between cubicles has created a new urgency. No longer are the cubicles cultural monoliths. Now, many cubicles contain representatives from many if not most of the other cubicles. What once seemed obvious is now murky, what once seemed certain is now ambiguous. Ethnocentric values that once dominated are now viewed with suspicion. There are feelings of threat, excitement, anticipation, fear and ambiguity in many. This very mix of feelings leaves ambiguity where there was once certainty.

Some tentative explorations for sharing perspectives with each other have begun. Much needs to be learned and tried before there will be confidence that such sharing is even possible. Meanwhile, the sculpture continues to subtly change. Each of the cubicles is increasingly unsure what these changes imply. Some insist that the changes only confirm what they already know, while others feel deeply threatened and suspicious. Some even insist that the change is being caused by "those strangers" and it would be best if they returned from whence they came.

The Fluid Sculpture can be whatever you want it to be. For me it is the representation of the human knowledge of God. Even within the church, within congregations we have difficulty seeing beyond the bounds of our own cubicles. We disrespect each other as a result of theological disagreements and we staunchly defend the perspective of our own cubicle as being the one and only true perspective. We have much work to do.

CHAPTER TEN

Consequences of Racism

The task of reconciliation is not complete until the consequences of racism are addressed. We may apologize and seek to end racism, but until we address these consequences our actions are little more than nice words that African Americans have heard for generations. The consequences continue to impair, frustrate and build resentment. The pain and hurt continue to damage and deny equality and respect. There has been discussion regarding reparations for slavery, which certainly would be appropriate, but may still not address these consequences. Reconciliation will be complete only when we have found the ways to address and redress these consequences.

We may have difficulty identifying all of these issues. We will be required to elicit that information from African Americans and have them affirm our definitions of those issues. We can and need to, however, begin to develop a list that will help us begin to focus out attention and develop appropriate strategies. The following list is not assumed to be complete, but is intended to begin our conversations.

Differing Perceptions of Current Events

The perspectives of African Americans are deeply influenced by their experience of injustice for centuries. The very assumptions that White people make which they see as foundational are often not shared by African Americans. These perspectives are often a continuing point of division and mistrust. For example, many African Americans defend O. J. Simpson as a victim of prosecution because he was a very successful Black man. They are convinced that the police framed Simpson. White people assume that Simpson is guilty and he got away with it because he had the money and influence to hire powerful lawyers. The same phenomenon has taken place as Barry Bonds broke the home run record in baseball. White people tend to believe he is guilty of taking steroids and many African Americans believe he has been set up and is being treated unjustly.

This consequence in which African Americans do not believe or trust the justice system of the United States is certainly understandable. Confidence will not be built until the justice system is able to consistently demonstrate impartial and equal justice. This will not take place until we listen to their experience and address the inequality they have experienced.

Criminal Justice and juvenile justice disparity

Why is it that a White person arrested in possession of cocaine may not serve any jail time while a Black young person in possession of a small amount of crack cocaine will be sentenced for a long time in jail? Why does racial profiling continue? Why do Black shoppers experience being followed in department stores?

Continued de facto segregation

White people and African Americans tend not to live in the same neighborhoods nor do they tend to freely socialize. Relationships that allow personal conversation and natural friendships are not common. Misunderstanding and misperception thrive due to this lack of relationships. These relationships are essential to develop free flowing conversation and dialogue. Economic development and family income are the primarily forces that continue this segregation. Public schools in poor Black communities do not have the same quality of education in affluent White neighborhoods. The educational system tends to trap Black young people in their ability to achieve economic success and thus the cycle continues.

Ten South African Insights

Upon returning from South Africa in 1999, I wrote this list of ten most important ideas I learned. Reflect on the application of these to our experience in the United States.

1. Racism is empowered through denial. When we deny we are a racist society, we empower racism. Racism in South Africa is disempowered because it is recognized and made public. It has been named and exposed.

2. The Gospel can be applied to a secular society and thereby change that society. The Truth and Reconciliation Commission was born in the church, lead by the church, and the society has begun to heal through the leadership of the church.

3. Only victims can offer grace, and when they do the Grace of God overcomes all hatred and behaviors even when the victims have been brutalized. Revenge is not the only option, though it is usually the option chosen.

4. Racism exacts a heavy cost on society. Racism erodes societies from the core. Even a repressive and controlled society finally collapsed as racism destroyed it.

5. The sins of the fathers are visited upon their children. The consequences of racism must be paid by those who come after it is ended. This may not be fair, but consequences require solutions regardless of the feelings or convictions of those who inherit them.

6. Bridge people are crucial, and those who live out their spirituality on both sides of the bridge will redeem the situation. Bridge people commit themselves to live on both sides of the river.

7. When facing apparent insurmountable problems we will feel overwhelmed by the magnitude of the task before us. We must remember that our task is to create small pockets of hope in the midst of desperation. Someday those small pockets will connect and the insurmountable problems will be resolved.

8. Guilt leads to fear which leads to brutality which leads to guilt. This cycle is broken only when grace is given by the victims of the brutality. The cycle is renewed each time revenge is chosen and grace is rejected.

9. Multiethnic community requires honesty, integrity, respect and lots of good humor. Multiethnic community requires that we listen carefully, and not take ourselves too seriously.

10. Miracles happen! The apartheid government represented less than ten percent of the population of South Africa. Ninety percent of the populations were oppressed by ten percent during apartheid. When the oppression ended, the oppressed took power and a blood bath of revenge was expected. They did not choose revenge. As one of them said, "An atrocity of the past will not be corrected by an atrocity in the present or future. Atrocities are corrected by doing what is right. We have forgiven them."

POSTSCRIPT

Privilege is unknown to those who have it,
Resented by those who do not.
Privilege is not earned by work or achievement.
Those who don't have it can't gain it by work or
achievement.
Denial of privilege fans the embers of resentment to flames
of infuriation in those who are oppressed by it.
Privilege provides comfort without discipline or effort,
while those without privilege yearn for small conveniences.
Privilege is assured and demanded by the egos it creates,
while demeaning the self respect of those who dare not
make demands.
Privilege weakens the fabric of community,
ease is valued more than challenge or struggle.
Strength is born in those without privilege as they seek
community.
Privilege seeks happiness, enjoyment and success
at the expense of those who are denied due respect.
Privilege allows waste of food and clothing,
while children die from starvation and cold.
Privilege gives us our wealth and our happiness,
while it gives us failure and shame.
May we soon give up our privilege that we might find life
that is whole.

Boyd Stockdale

Taylor Stockdale read the following poem at the memorial service for his father, my cousin, Vice Admiral James Stockdale. This poem was found on the wall of a prison following the Civil War and was written by an anonymous prisoner of war. Being a POW during the Vietnam War himself, this was one of Jim's favorite poems.

We asked for strength that we might achieve,
God made us weak that we might obey.
We asked for health that we might do great things,
He gave us infirmity that we might do better things.
We asked for riches that we might be happy,
We were given poverty that we might be wise.
We asked for power that we might have the praise of men,
We were given weakness that we might feel the need of God.
We asked for all things that we might enjoy life,
We were given life that we might enjoy all things.
We received nothing that we asked for,
But all we that we hoped
And our prayers were answered,
We are most blessed.

Anonymous

May it be so.

ACKNOWLEDGEMENTS

My wife, Susan, lived this process with me for forty years. She has given strength, encouragement and insight. Without her, this project may have remained only in my thoughts and never written. She has kept it all in perspective which has provided us the opportunity to reflect and learn together.

Rudy Cuellar pushed me into the reconciliation process before I even knew I needed it and certainly before I desired it. I visited Rudy in Sacramento in 2007. I had not seen him since 1970. He continues to be a wonderful gift to me.

Daisy Dawson, Gladys Edelton, Fordy and Thelma Ross, who tried one more time to tell their experiences as Black Presbyterians in Seattle, took the risk of being rejected one more time. They taught me the difficulty and the power of reconciliation.

Family members, my sister Phyllis McCall and our daughter Lisa McPherson, edited, critiqued, supported, and encouraged.

Editors Lisa Konick edited a very early draft which helped me establish some order in the midst of the chaos, and Lucy Kellogg Farley found all of those mistakes that continued to hide from those of us who had failed to see them too many times.

The fifty people who participated in the Race in America Class at Mercer Island Presbyterian Church tested *Conflict vs. Survival* as a resource to understand and defeat racism.

Without Ben Sherman, Cielo Press, this book would still be a manuscript in a three ring binder. His willingness to apply his skill and ability to this project is greatly appreciated.

BIBLIOGRAPHY

Akbar, Na'im *Breaking the Chains of Psychological Slavery*.
Tallahassee, Fl: Mind Productions and Associates, 2002

Althen, Gary. *American Ways: A Guide for Foreigners in the United States*. Yarmouth, Maine: Intercultural Press, 1988.

Anderson, Alita. *On the Other Side: African Americans Tell of Healing*.
Louisville, Westminster John Knox Press, 2001.

Ashe, Geoffrey. *The Discovery of King Arthur*. New York: Henry Holt and Company, 1985.

Bennett, Jr., Lerone. *Before the Mayflower: A history of the Negro in America 1619-1964*. Baltimore: Penguin Books, 1966.

Bennett, Jr., Lerone. *The Shaping of Black America*. New York: Penguin Books, 1993.

Black, Edwin. *War Against the Weak: Eugenics and America's Campaign to Create a Master Race*. New York. Four Walls Eight Windows, 2003.

Browder, Anthony T. *From the Browder File*. Washington, D.C. The Institute of Karmic Guidance, 2002.

Brown, Robert McAfee. *Making Peace in the Global Village*.
Philadelphia: Westminster Press. 1981.

Bulfinch, Thomas. *Bulfinch's Mythology*. New York, Modern Library. Random House, Inc.

Chesterton, G. K. *Eugenics and Other Evils: An Argument Against the Scientifically Organized Society*. Seattle: Inkling Books. 2001.

Dalton, Harlon L. *Racial Healing: Confronting the Fear Between Blacks and Whites*. New York, Anchor Books, 1996.

DeYoung, Curtiss Paul and others. *United by Faith: The Multiracial Congregation as an Answer to the Problem of Race*. Oxford: Oxford University Press. 2003.

Douglass, Frederick. *My Bondage and My Freedom*. New York, Penguin Books, 2003.

Emerson, Michael O. and others. *Divided by Faith: Evangelical Religion and the Problem of Race in America*. Oxford: Oxford University Press, 2000.

Ezekiel, Raphael S. *The Racist Mind: Portraits of American Neo-Nazis and Klansmen*. New York, Viking/Penguin. 1995.

Green, Roger Lancelyn. *King Arthur and His Knights of the Round Table*. London. Puffin Books. 1953

Hale-Benson, Janice E. *Black Children; Their Roots, Culture, and Learning Styles*. Baltimore. The Johns Hopkins University Press.1986

Harris, Joseph E. *Africans and Their History*. New York. New American Library, Penguin Books. 1972

Hilliard, David. *Strangers and Pilgrims*. Bryn Mawr, Buy Books on the Web.com. 1988.

Howarth-Williams, Maartin. *R. D. Laing: His Work and its Relevance for Sociology*. London. Routledge and Kegan Paul. 1977.

Laband, John. The *Rise and Fall of the Zulu Nation*. London, Arms and Armour, 1997.

Lamb, Harold. *The Crusades*. New York. Bantam Books. 1962.

Laing, R. D. *Interpersonal Perception: A Theory and a Method of Research*. New York. Perennial Library, Harper and Row. 1972

Leary, Joy DeGruy. *Post Traumatic Slave Syndrome*.Milwaukie, Oregon. Uptone Press, 2005

Price, Frederick K. C. *Race, Religion and Racism: A Bold Encounter With Division in the Church*. Los Angeles. Faith One Publishing. 1999.

Probe John S. and Onsite II, Gabriel. *African Initiatives in Christianity: The Growth, Gifts and Diversities of Indigenous African Churches*. Geneva, WCC Publications, 1998

Richardson, E. Allen. *Strangers in This Land: Pluralism and the Response to Diversity in the United States*. New York. Pilgrim Press. 1988.

Rodney, Walter. *How Europe Underdeveloped Africa*. Washington D. C. Howard University Press. 1982.

Smith, Gary. *Radical Compassion: Finding Christ in the Heart of the Poor*. Chicago. Loyola Press. 2002.

Stockdale, Jim and Sybil. *In Love and War: the story of a family's ordeal and sacrifice during the Vietnam years*. New York, Harper and Row Publishers, 1984

Takaki, Ronald. *From Different Shores: Perspectives on Race and Ethnicity in America*. Oxford. Oxford University Press. 1987

Tutu, Desmond. *No Future Without Forgiveness*. New York. Doubleday, First Image Books. 2000.

Upton, Robert. *Racism @ Work Among the Lord's People*. Tulsa. Insight Publishers. 2003

West, Cornell. *Race Matters*. New York. Random House, Vintage Books. 1993.

Woodson, Carter G. *The Miss-education of the Negro*. London. Africa World Press. 1998.

Periodicals and Articles

African American Platform. Chicago, April 30, 2004.

Arunga, Marsha Tate. *The Stolen Ones.* Seattle Post Intelligencer, July 8, 2001

Arunga, Marsha Tate. Cultural Reconnection for African American Women. Literature Review of Thesis.

Brewster, Charles E. We Must Find Ways of Working Together. Presbyterian Outlook, Volume 181. May 3, 1999.

Carnes, Jim. *Us and Them: A History of Intolerance in America.* Teaching Tolerance, A Project of the Southern Poverty Law Center.1995

Crichton, Michael. *Why Politicized Science is Dangerous (Excerpted from State of Fear).* MichaelCrichton.com March 10, 2007

Encarta Africana. *What is Kwanzaa? African American Watch Night Service*

Lee, Luna Chang-Ran. F*acing Racism: In Search of the Beloved Community.* Louisville: Presbyterian Peacemaking Program. Presbyterian Church, U.S.A. 1998

Crossroads Ministry. *An Interfaith and Community Based Anti-Racism Training Organization: New Models to Dismantle Racism and Build Anti-racist Multicultural Diversity in Institutions and Communities.* Chicago. 1996

Goodheart, Adam. *Change of Heart.* AARP The Magazine. May/June 2004.

Habersham, David. *Shall We Overcome?* Parade Magazine, Seattle Times, April 18, 2004.

Herbert, Bob. *Main Goal of Brown v. Board Has Been Thwarted by Regresses.* Seattle Post Intelligencer. April 27, 2004.

Howell, Leon. *Using Private Lynch.* Christian Century, December 13, 2000.

Jensen, Robert. *Personal Voices: The Good White People.* AlterNet May 4, 2004. Received from Bailey de Inch, Manager, King County Civil Rights, Seattle, Washington.

Law, Eric H. E. *Living the Gospel of Peace.* Louisville: Presbyterian Peacemaking Program, Presbyterian Church U.S.A. 2004

Littleton, Scott C. and Malcor, Linda A. *Some Notes on Merlin.* Los Angeles. Occidental College. 1994

Loma, Mark A. *Reparations: Getting to Ground Level.* Presbyterian Women. Presbyterian Church U.S.A. Louisville: Horizons Magazine. November/December 2004.

National Council of Churches. *Urban Strategy Resources: Witnessing to the Gospel, Tools for Racial Justice*. New York. Peace work. February 1991

Slavery was hot topic at Last Richmond General Assembly. PCUSA News. June 26, 2004.

Elton, Lee M. *Brown v. Board: Protecting a legacy of social justice and equality*. Seattle Times May 16, 2004.

Smith, Margaret D. *The Call to Reconciliation: John Perkins Brings His Legacy to SPU*. Response. Seattle Pacific University. Autumn 2004.

Stockdale, Boyd. *The Japanese Experience in the American Church*. Unpublished. Sacramento, Synod of the Pacific. 1992

Warlik, Nancy. *In The Mood for Prejudice?* King County Journal. April 24, 2004

Wise, Tim ZNET Daily Commentaries Many, many valuable resource articles by Tim Wise.

United to End Racism. *Working Together to End Racism: Healing from the Damage Caused by Racism*. Seattle: Rational Island Publishers. 2001

Willowbrook Report, Lausanne Committee for World Evangelism, 1978, www.lausanne.org/willowbrook.1978/lop-2

ENDNOTES

[1] Lerone Bennett, Jr,.*The Shaping of Black America* (New York: Penguin Books, 1993) p.61

[2] Ibid.p.73

[3] Ibid. p.212

[4] Desmond Tutu, *No Future Without Forgiveness* (New York: Doubleday 2000) p.217

[5] Ashe, Geoffrey, *The Discovery of King Arthur*. New York, Henry Holt and Company, 1985 p.190

[6] Ibid .p 123

[7] Ibid. p.192

[8] Edwin Black, *War Against The Weak* (New York: Four Walls/Eight Windows, 2003) p.31

[9] Ibid. p.38

[10] Ibid. p.163

[11] Ibid p.411

[12] Ibid p.412

[13] G. K. Chesterton, *Eugenics and Other Evils* (Seattle: Inkling Books, 2000) p.29

[14] Rudyard Kipling Poems. www.poetryloverspage.com/poets/kipling

[15] Brinkley, Alan. *American History, A Survey. Volume I.* 9th ed. (New York: McGraw-Hill 1995) p.352

[16] Stockdale, Jim and Sybil, *In Love and War* (New York: Harper and Row Publishers, 1984) p.23

[17] ibid. p.23

[18] Na'im Akbar, Breaking the Chains of Psychological Slavery (Tallahassee, Fl: Mind Productions and Associates, 2002) p.14

[19] Ibid. p.17

[20] Loren Bennett, op.cit, p.116

[21] Akbar, op. cit. p.15

[22] Akbar, op. cit. p.18

[23] Akbar, op.cit. p.18

[24] Janice E. Hale-Benson, *Black Children* (Baltimore: Johns Hopkins University Press, 1986) p.61

[25] The Institute of Karmic Guidance, 2000) p.77

[26] Ibid. p.77

[27] From a paper by Edwin J. Nichols, Clinical/Industrial Psychologist, Washington. D.C. 1985

[28] Woodson, Carter G. *The Mis-education of the Negro*. London. Africa World Press. 1998 p. xii

[29] Tutu, op.cit. p.35

[30] Browder, op.cit p,77

[31] Laing, R. D. *Interpersonal Perception: A theory and Method of Research*. New York. Perennial Library, Harper and Row, 1972. p. 3

[32] Ibid. p.5

[33] Ibid. p.6

[34] Tutu op. cit. p.35

[35] Laing op. cit. p.35

[36] Harlon L. Dalton. *Racial Healing, Confronting the Fear between Blacks and Whites* (New York: Anchor Books) p. 15

[37] Ibid. p.53

[38] Ibid. p.55

[39] Ibid. p.73

[41] Ibid. p. 29

[42] Ezekiel, Raphael S. *The Racist Mind: Portraits of American Neo Nazis and Klansmen*. New York, Viking/Penguin 1995 p.xix

[43] Ibid. p. xviii

[44] Ibid. p. xviii

[45] Structural Review of Presbyterian Women from an Antiracism Perspective. Background For Study, www.pcusa.org

[46] Presbyterian Women, Task Group Report and Recommendations, Perceptions of Racism, wwwpcusa.org

[47] Ibid, Changes in Communication and Training

[48] Ibid, Changes in Communication and Training

[49] Ibid. Lack of Willingness to Change

[50] General Assembly News Service, June 9, 2003 John Filiatreau.

[51] Emerson, Michael and others. *Divided by Faith: Evangelical Religion and the Problem of Race in America*, Oxford University Press, 2000. p.1

[52] Ibid. p.29

[53] Ibid. p. 89